a
road
guide
to the
geology
of
big
bend
national
park

kerri nelson

Copyright 1992 by Big Bend Natural History Association
ISBN 0-912001-15-1
Editors: Robert Rothe, Rick Louis LoBello
Design: Sandra McKee
Production: Rick Louis LoBello
Lithography: Paragon Press
Artwork: All drawings not credited are by Cindy Parr.
    Mike Anderson: 12 map, 56 Lone Mountain
    Lawrence Ormsby: 26 Casa Grande, 46 Santa Elena Canyon
Photographs: All photographs not credited are from the files of Big Bend
National Park and the National Park Service.
    Rick Louis LoBello: 15, 19, 25, 33, 40, 42, 44, 46, 50, 51, 56, 61,
    63, 65

Dedication

*This book is dedicated to all those who
have experienced and enjoyed Big Bend National Park.*

Acknowledgements

I wish to thank the Big Bend Natural History Association for providing me the opportunity to compile this book and the staff of Big Bend National Park for their collective assistance and encouragement. I would especially like to thank Robert Rothe, Chief of Interpretation and Visitor Services, for his continual encouragement and guidance during all preparations of this book. He willingly contributed his time and suggestions, both of which facilitated completion of the manuscript.

Special thanks is also extended to the following individuals who critically reviewed the manuscript: Karen Boucher, Rick LoBello, Wayne Moore, Keith Reeves, Dennis Schucker and Carol Sperling.

Finally, I would also like to thank Dennis Nelson for his assistance in the field and significant contributions to the road logs.

Kerri Nelson

TABLE OF CONTENTS

USING THIS ROAD LOG: Roadside mile posts may not always exactly concur with the mileage on your odometer. Watch for these mile posts and make adjustments as necessary. Numbers in bold represent distance between stops and slow down areas. Roadside stops are also described.

GLOSSARY: terms highlighted in bold are defined in the glossary.

COLLECTING: Because national parks were established to protect the land and to leave everything within their boundaries unimpaired for the enjoyment of future generations, the collecting or disturbing of rocks, cacti and other plants, animals, or historic or prehistoric artifacts is prohibited.

MAKE SAFETY YOUR CONSTANT COMPANION: The road logs that follow describe the geology of the park at both designated stops and stretches of road described as "slow down areas." If you are driving alone at these points you will need to pull off the road and stop to read the text safely.

You will find it helpful to have additional maps of the park with you as a companion to this road guide. Some may prefer the shaded relief topographic map of the park. A geologic map of the park is contained in "The Big Bend of the Rio Grande," Guidebook 7, by Ross A. Maxwell, Bureau of Economic Geology/The University of Texas at Austin, 1968. Both publications can be obtained from the Big Bend Natural History Association.

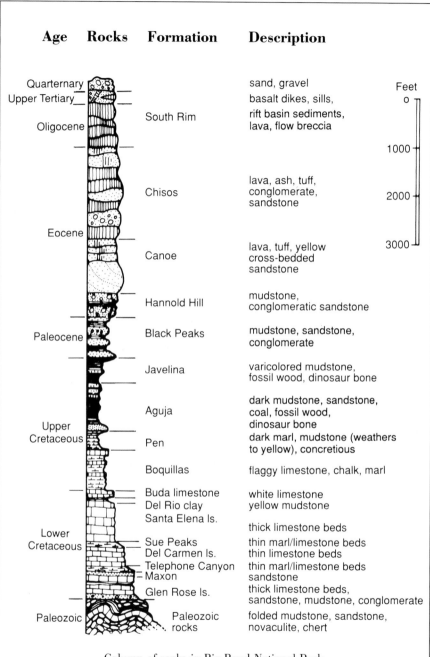

Age	Rocks	Formation	Description

Age   **Rocks**   **Formation**   **Description**

Quarternary — sand, gravel

Upper Tertiary — basalt dikes, sills,

Oligocene — South Rim — rift basin sediments, lava, flow breccia

Chisos — lava, ash, tuff, conglomerate, sandstone

Eocene

Canoe — lava, tuff, yellow cross-bedded sandstone

Hannold Hill — mudstone, conglomeratic sandstone

Paleocene — Black Peaks — mudstone, sandstone, conglomerate

Javelina — varicolored mudstone, fossil wood, dinosaur bone

Aguja — dark mudstone, sandstone, coal, fossil wood, dinosaur bone

Upper Cretaceous

Pen — dark marl, mudstone (weathers to yellow), concretious

Boquillas — flaggy limestone, chalk, marl

Buda limestone — white limestone

Del Rio clay — yellow mudstone

Santa Elena ls. — thick limestone beds

Lower Cretaceous

Sue Peaks — thin marl/limestone beds

Del Carmen ls. — thin limestone beds

Telephone Canyon — thin marl/limestone beds

Maxon — sandstone

Glen Rose ls. — thick limestone beds, sandstone, mudstone, conglomerate

Paleozoic — Paleozoic rocks — folded mudstone, sandstone, novaculite, chert

Feet
0
1000
2000
3000

Column of rocks in Big Bend National Park.

INTRODUCTION

The geology of Big Bend National Park records a varied and dynamic history. Ancient rocks, bent and twisted by **tectonic** forces deep within the Earth, now pierce the valley floors and form mountain ranges; towering limestone cliffs, replete with the fossils of myriad sea creatures, are sediments from an ancient sea; jagged spires of **igneous** rock bear testimony to volcanic activity that raged here eons ago.

The vast expanse of the Big Bend country can appear changeless — a region frozen in time. But in reality, processes are continually working to reshape the topography of the Big Bend landscape. Some of these processes, such as **sediment** deposition or erosion, are ongoing, either building new rock layers or stripping them away. **Volcanism**, once an enormous force for change, is now an inactive process. **Faulting, folding,** and mountain building **(orogeny)** slowly but with great force continue to shape rocks buried deep in the Earth, and in due course may rework the face of Big Bend again. But beyond these forces is a fourth dimension, time.

Geologic Time

Geologic time can be divided into four major episodes, listed in order from oldest to most recent: **Precambrian, Paleozoic, Mesozoic,** and **Cenozoic.** Based on **radiometric** dating of **meteorites**, geologists believe that our solar system is approximately 4.5 billion years old. However, the oldest rocks now exposed at the Earth's surface are 3.8 billion years old. Compared to these ancient rocks, the ones found in Big Bend are relatively young; the oldest rock exposed in the park is a mere 525 million years old. Still, for we who measure our lives in tens of years, and civilizations in hundreds of years, the concept of geologic time often is difficult to grasp. To get a feeling for the enormity of geologic time, you can compare geologic time to one Earth year. Using January first to mark the beginning of our solar system, imagine life first appearing in late May and humans, relative late-comers, arriving in the last four minutes of the year. In fact, (in this model), most of our recorded history fits neatly into the last few seconds of the year.

Whatever we know about Earth history we learn from information recorded in the rocks. Each of the processes that form rocks puts its "print" in the rocks. For example, sediments deposited in the sea will contain the shells of marine creatures whereas sediments deposited by streams will contain fossils of fresh water creatures, land animals and fossil wood. Geologists are trained to "read" the "prints" left by the various processes that have occurred to produce the Earth we see today. Just as flowing streams erode the Earth's surface, so did ancient streams. We find that the Earth has undergone continuous change since its beginning. So it is with the Big Bend region. **Paleozoic** strata, the oldest rocks exposed in the park, formed in a deep ocean basin hundreds of millions of years ago. From this beginning, the Big Bend region underwent several transformations to become the desert of today.

Introduction

Limestone.

The Paleozoic Era

Deep seas covered the Big Bend during the Paleozoic Era, more than 500 million years ago. The water-covered area, known as the **Ouachita** Trough, extended northeasterly into what is now Arkansas and Oklahoma and received vast quantities of sediment from the continent to the north. Abundant marine fossils, such as sponges, **graptolites,** brachiopods, and trilobites found in the rocks between Persimmon Gap and Marathon tell us about these seas. The **Maravillas,** Caballos, and Tesnus Formations were deposited in this sea and are exposed at Persimmon Gap. The rocks of these formations are **sedimentary,** predominantly **cherts, limestones,** and **shales,** and are characteristic of **deep-marine environments**. The sediments forming these rocks settled slowly through the **deep marine** waters and accumulated in horizontal layers on the ocean floor. Some sediments cascaded downslope in ancient underwater avalanches. With time and pressure these sediments **lithified,** forming rock layers.

Two important geologic principles, or laws, give perspective to the history of these Paleozoic rocks. The first law states that in any series of undisturbed stratified sedimentary rocks, the oldest strata are at the bottom and the youngest strata are at the top of the sequence. The second law states that when a sediment is deposited in water and settles to the sea floor, it tends to form horizontal layers. The layered **Paleozoic** rocks you will explore at Persimmon Gap stand warped and twisted, giving little evidence that they ever rested horizontally on an ancient sea floor. This lack of horizontality in these rocks records a major **tectonic event,** the Quachita Orogeny, that occurred during the Pennsylvanian Period near the close of the Paleozoic Era when the North American and South American **plates** collided with each other (about 250 million years ago). This orogeny folded the deep sea rocks and thrust them skyward, creating an ancient mountain range.

Introduction

The Mesozoic Era

During the early part of the following era, the Mesozoic Era, the mountains were eroded and no rocks recording the geologic history of the **Triassic** or **Jurassic** Periods are exposed in Big Bend. This gap in the rock record is called an **unconformity,** but it still provides us with useful information. Geologists believe that the Triassic and Jurassic Periods were times of intense erosion of the Paleozoic mountain ranges. The rocks eroded from these mountains were deposited in a Mesozoic sea.

Geologists can only infer what happened during the Early Mesozoic because there is no rock record preserved. However we do find rocks deposited during the **Cretaceous** Period of the Late Mesozoic Age. During that period, shallow seas, extending from the new Gulf of Mexico to Alaska, covered the area. Thick **limestones,** now exposed in the Sierra del Carmen and at Santa Elena Canyon, were deposited. The abundant fossils, mostly different kinds of mollusks, tell us that these were warm, moderately deep seas.

Later, in the Middle Cretaceous, the seas retreated and limestone beds became thinner, forming **flagstones** in the Boquillas Formation. These limestone beds alternated with clay beds that are now shale layers in the Pen Formation.

Late in the Cretaceous Period, the seas withdrew from the Big Bend area. **Terrestrial** fossils of dinosaurs, flying reptiles and trees were deposited in the **sandstones, siltstones** and shales of the Aguja and **Javelina Formations,** the most recent of the Mesozoic **sediments.** Fossils of the largest flying animal known, a reptile called "pterodactyl," originated from these beds. It had a wingspan of 35 to 38 feet (10.67 to 11.58 meters).

Also near the end of the Cretaceous and extending into the **Cenozoic** Era, tectonic forces of the **Laramide** Orogeny caused the folding and faulting that formed the Rocky Mountains and the Sierra Madre. While not as high as the mountains to the north and to the south, the Santiago Mountains north of the park, the Sierra del Carmen, and the Mariscal and San Vicente **anticline** are also part of the Rocky Mountain system. Thus the Laramide orogeny brought the Mesozoic Era to a close and set the stage for the volcanic activity of the **Cenozoic** Era.

The Cenozoic Era

Nonmarine sediments continued to be deposited in the Early Cenozoic, engulfing skeletal remains which became the oldest mammal fossils found in Texas. The Fossil Bone Exhibit, near the upper Tornillo Creek bridge contains replicas of bones from some of these extinct mammals.

Volcanic activity began about 38 million years ago and continued until about 20 million years ago; that is, from latest Eocene through Oligocene time. Two

Introduction

Laccolith.

major volcanoes, the Sierra Quemada Volcano followed by the Pine Canyon Volcano, dominated the mid-**Tertiary** skyline, flooding the land with **lava** and choking the sky with ash. Eruptions from these two volcanoes were similar to those at Mt. St. Helens, but on a much grander scale. In fact, both of the Big Bend volcanoes erupted so much material that the earth's surface collapsed, forming **calderas**. The lava and **ash** accumulated to great thicknesses and can be seen at such places as Cerro Castellan, Goat Mountain, Burro Mesa, and the cliffs on the South Rim of the Chisos Mountains.

In late Oligocene-early Miocene time, when tension in the earth's crust became significant, **magma intrusions** in the form of **dikes, laccoliths** and **plugs** intruded the **Mesozoic** and Cenozoic sediments and volcanic rocks. These intrusions remained underground until erosion uncovered them. One such intrusion is Pulliam Peak, located in the Basin.

Tension on the crust increased some 20 million years ago and normal **faulting** of the Basin and Range style began forming a series of basins **(grabens)** and mountain ranges **(horsts)**. The central portion of the park, between the Santiago Mountains to the east and the Mesa de Anguila and Sierra Ponce on the southwest, dropped down. We call the downward section the Sunken Block. Faulting developed in the Sierra del Carmen and the Sunken Block as well. These intrusions marked the end of **igneous** activity in Big Bend.

Since the Pleistocene, erosion has been the dominant force sculpting the Big Bend country, deepening canyons and hewing rough-shaped mountains into mesas. Water, the most effective tool of erosion, continues to be, in both dramatic and subtle ways, the major force shaping and molding the face of Big Bend. Although this is an arid land, a summer thunderstorm may produce a deluge in less than an hour. Flood waters rushing down arroyos excavate and reposition huge boulders, demonstrating the awesome power of water. Meanwhile, raindrops, dislodging small rock particles, etch canyon walls and mountainsides.

The basins formed by faulting filled with debris eroded from the Chisos Mountains, the Sierra del Carmen, and other **uplifted** ridges. As the Rio Grande developed its channel, erosion shaped the landforms we see today: lava capped mesas

Introduction

Ancient volcano.

and buttes, hogbacks around **intrusions,** and dike ridges. More resistant igneous intrusions formed mountains and high hills like Ward, Vernon Bailey, and Pulliam peaks, Elephant Tusk, Grapevine Hills, and McKinney Hills. Resistant dikes, intruded into the **tuffs** of the Chisos Formation and have since been exposed by erosion. Impressive examples of these dikes, including the Mule Ears, can be seen along the Ross Maxwell Scenic Drive.

The original land level of the land surface was above today's highest peaks in the Chisos Mountains and highest cliffs of the Mesa de Anguila. As the Rio Grande channeled deeper it cut through the resistant **Cretaceous limestones** to form the deep canyons of Santa Elena, Mariscal, Boquillas and the Lower Canyons.

The extensive surfaces, **pediments** and **alluvial fans,** that slope away from the Chisos Mountains and other high areas are products of the continuing erosion cycle. As the region became more arid, erosion resulted mostly from the **sheet flow** that accompanies the rare but intense thunderstorms that occur during the summer months. This rapid erosion and deposition causes the surface to be covered with extensive gravel deposits best seen in road cuts, a fitting cap to a complex geologic picture.

Big Bend is a veritable laboratory of geologic phenomena. **Volcanism, faulting, folding,** mountain building and erosion are part of the park's geologic legacy outlined in the roadlogs which follow. Discover through these pages the geologic anatomy of vast vistas, upthrust mountain masses, and stark eroded landscapes, a topography that both challenges the mind and consoles the spirit.

This brief guide is merely an introduction to the geology of Big Bend National Park. For more detailed information on the geology of Big Bend consult the bibliography on page 75 .

Panther Junction to Boquillas Canyon

Sierra del Carmen mountain range near Rio Grande Village.

Panther Junction to Boquillas Canyon

Panther Junction to Boquillas Canyon
(Suggested travel time: late afternoon)
24.6 miles one way

The **Cretaceous** Period, a time of shallow seas, swamps, marshes and **deltas,** left a rich record in the rocks of Big Bend. Today you will see **sedimentary** rocks, both **clastic** (e.g. **sandstones**) and chemical (e.g. **limestone**), that record this Cretaceous history, as well as other geologic features that add to the intriguing geologic story of Big Bend.

Mileage Reading
0.00 Panther Junction Park Headquarters. Set your odometer to zero at the road junction.

.80

.80 **Stop 1.** Park on shoulder.
Exposed on the right side of the road is a **ring dike,** an intrusive **igneous** rock that frequently forms when a volcano collapses, creating a **caldera.** The pillar-like rocks, formed by **columnar jointing,** originated when **magma** cooled and con-tracted. Subsequently, pieces of the columns broke off, collecting around the base of dike. Why have these columns broken down? Water freezing and thawing in the spaces between the columns have forced the rock to shift, crack and crumble during infrequent winter storms and subfreezing temperatures. As thawing pro-gressed, even larger cracks developed, allowing more water to accumulate. Several such cycles eventually dislodged large portions of rock from the ring dike. Note the red, orange, and black stains on the dike rock, more evidence that water is attack-ing the rock face. Through chemical reactions involving water, minerals in the dike have been dissolved while red and orange iron oxides as well as black manganese oxide stains have been deposited. Staining like this is a surface phenomenon because solid, unfractured rock prohibits deep penetration of water. Consequently, the face of a rock may become highly altered but its interior remains original and unstained.

.35

1.15 **Stop 2.** Park on shoulder.
To the right Pummel, Wright, and Panther peaks and the Panther **Laccolith** domi-nate the landscape. Beneath these promontories lie the layered **tuffs** of the Chisos Formation.

Panther Junction to Boquillas Canyon

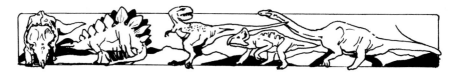

Limestone face of the Sierra del Carmen overshadowing McKinney Hills and alluvial deposits, mile 1.15.

To the far left the dark-colored intrusive rocks of the McKinney Hills rise just above the desert floor. Behind the low, rolling McKinney Hills stands the limestone face of the Sierra del Carmen, also called the Deadhorse Mountains. In the immediate foreground are **alluvial** deposits. **Alluvial fans** formed from material stripped off the surrounding hillsides. Where two or more fans merge, a **bajada** forms. **Erosion** plays a major role in shaping the landscape: look for more **bajadas** throughout Big Bend.

.55

1.70 **Slow down area.**
The low, **rubbly** ridge to the left in the immediate foreground is another **ring dike,** a remnant of the violent **igneous** history of the Big Bend country.

.60

2.30 **Stop 3.** Park on shoulder.
While viewing Pummel Peak to the right, you have a good opportunity to compare the igneous rocks of the South Rim and Chisos Formations. The massive grayish South Rim Formation rocks lie on top of the reddish brown Chisos Formation rocks exposed in the slopes. Why do these two formations, composed entirely of igneous rocks, appear so differently from one another? In essence, the South Rim rocks seen here are all **ash** flows. These ash flows, often erupting in glowing avalanches of extremely hot, dense material, were through time **welded** together to form massive, resistant cliffs. In contrast, the Chisos Formation exposed here consists of a less resistant series of thinly-bedded **air**

Ring dike, mile 1.70.

14

fall tuffs, reworked tuffs, and **lava flows**. Unlike the South Rim Formation, none of the Chisos Formation rocks formed massive cliffs. Instead they readily eroded to form slopes. This combination of cliffs and slopes formed through **differential erosion,** a dynamic process that played an important role in producing the varied and striking landscape of Big Bend. Differential erosion occurs widely throughout the park and is not restricted to igneous rocks. In fact, as you continue this trip you will see examples of differential erosion among various **limestone** rocks.

Phenocrysts, mile 2.70.

.50

2.80 **Stop 4.** Park on shoulder near the large rocks on the right.

The ring dike exposed in the roadcut on the right appears different from the one you observed at Stop 1. Here the ring dike contains large mineral grains **(phenocrysts)** of clear and glassy quartz and chalky white **alkali feldspar.** Geologists refer to dikes containing these kinds of **silica-rich** minerals as rhyolitic dikes.

Notice also that parts of the outcrop are covered with a whitish crust of **caliche,** a mineral that frequently forms on rock surfaces in arid environments. Unlike quartz and alkali feldspar which originated and grew in the **magma** as primary minerals, caliche deposits developed long after the rock itself was formed and, therefore, is referred to as a secondary mineral. Look for white coatings of caliche on other rock surfaces.

Caliche, mile 2.70.

1.45

4.25 **Slow down area.**

Nugent Mountain.

Nugent Mountain (right) and the small hills in the immediate foreground are all intrusive rocks. Intrusive rocks solidify beneath the earth's surface. Here **erosion** of the overlying rock layers unearthed these intrusives and exposed them as mountains. What were the preexisting rocks that have long since been removed? They were probably **Tertiary**-age igneous rocks of the South Rim and Chisos Formations and **sediments** of the Canoe Formation. Perhaps even some **Cretaceous**-age rocks, like the **Javelina Formation,** were swept away to uncover these **intrusions**. The next obvious question, "What happened to the preexisting rock?", can, in part, be answered by looking around. The **alluvial fans** and gravel deposits hold many fragments of these rocks while others have been carried downstream by the Rio Grande.

2.25

6.50 Dugout Wells Road on the left.

1.10

7.60 **Slow down area**. Elephant Tusk Viewpoint.
From this vantage point you can see the blunt point of the Elephant Tusk intrusive jutting skyward (right). **Erosion,** stripping away the overlying rock, uncovered the peak. However, Elephant Tusk is not exempt from erosion and is continually being assailed. Only the rates of erosion differ between the intrusion and the softer surrounding rocks.

*Elephant Tusk,
mile 7.60.*

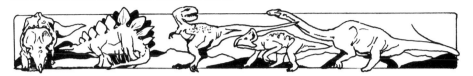

1.70

5.80

9.30 **Stop 5.** Park on pullout and get out of your vehicle.

Chilicotal Mountain (right) is composed of the Cretaceous-age Javelina Formation, capped by an igneous intrusion. If it weren't for the hard, resistant igneous cap rocks, Chilicotal Mountain probably would not exist. The soft, easily eroded sediments would have been stripped away long ago.

Erosion, though a less spectacular process than a volcanic eruption, is no less important in shaping the landscape. Over millions of years, erosive forces have waged a winning war against towering mountains, slowly breaking them down into smaller and smaller fragments. Subject to the forces of gravity and water, these fragments subsequently formed the **talus deposits** and **alluvial fans** that now blanket both mountain slopes and the desert floor. Ironically, while erosion can level the highest peaks it can also uncover rock formations long buried beneath overlying layers.

You are standing on an alluvial deposit. Look at some of the rock fragments and try to determine if they are primarily igneous or **sedimentary**. The type of rocks in the alluvium tells a great deal about the source area for the deposit. Here, the rocks are dominantly igneous, derived from the surrounding hills. Alluvial deposits are common throughout the park. In fact, the small, rounded hills (left) are constructed from deposits of alluvium.

You are driving on alluvial fan deposits. Can you locate **bajadas** on the near and far slopes?

15.10 **Stop 6.** Park on shoulder.

Exposed on the far right are outcrops of the **Cretaceous** sedimentary units which comprise the **Aguja Formation** containing mostly **clastic sandstones, siltstones** and **mudstone** formed from the breakdown of preexisting rocks. These clastic rocks also contain large pieces of dinosaur and tree fossils, indicating that the Aguja sediments were deposited near an ancient Cretaceous shore, perhaps even in a **delta** or lagoon. Why do geologists believe this to be true? It would be unlikely to find these large fossil fragments great distances from shore without having been shattered into smaller pieces along the way.

.90

16.00 **Stop 7.** At the River Road turnoff drive approximately .13 mile down the River Road and park on the left. The 4-wheel drive only sign applies only to that section of road beyond this point (note your odometer reading).

This stop provides an excellent opportunity to examine the **Aguja Formation** on the right. Look closely at the Aguja and note that the **sandstone** is the dominant **clastic** rock. Sandstones are formed in desert environments where wind deposited sand grains and in beach environments, where water aided sand deposition. When geologists investigate outcrops like these, they are looking for features that may be keys to unlocking the geologic story held within the rock.

17

Here two types of **sedimentary** structures are evident: ripple marks and **cross-bedding**. Either wind or water can work to form these features. The rock surfaces are littered with fossils, such as clams, and trace fossils, such as **burrows**. These features are the clues geologists use to reconstruct the history of a rock unit. For instance, the presence of sandstone, ripple marks, cross-bedding, and fossils all point to the Aguja Formation forming in a beach environment, perhaps a tidal flat. **Return to the main park road (adjust your odometer reading).**

.30

16.30 Lower Tornillo Creek Bridge.

.30

16.60 **Stop 8.** Park on shoulder just across the bridge.
As you look ahead, the Boquillas Formation crops out on the right side of the road and the yellow and white Pen Formation crops out on the left side. A normal Basin and Range fault has placed younger rocks adjacent to older rocks. The rocks to the left have sunk relative to those to the right. The road passes over the fault. The Boquillas Formation is composed of alternating **clastic (shale)** and chemical **(limestone)** beds. The shale erodes faster than the limestone, causing the more resistant limestone beds to stand out. These resistant layers, characteristic of the Boquillas Formation, are called **flagstones**.
Contrast the Boquillas **flagstone** with the massive cliffs of Santa Elena **Limestone** seen up ahead at Stop 11. The Santa Elena Limestone consists solely of

limestone, a chemical **sedimentary** rock formed through precipitation of calcium **carbonate** ($CaCO_3$) from solution. Most of the calcium forming these cliffs came from microscopic organisms that floated in the **Cretaceous** seas. When these minute creatures died, they sank slowly through the water. Their skeletons accumulated on the sea floor, providing the calcium to form limestones. These impressive cliffs owe much of their height to creatures too small to be seen with the unaided eye!

Here is another chance to observe close up, how different rocks erode. Crumbly **shales** and **siltstones** of the Pen Formation have been deeply incised by small rivulets that formed during intense rainfall. On the other hand, the thin-bedded harder Boquillas Formation appears smooth and rounded because the water could not quickly cut through the limestone. Instead, it cascaded over the beds, slowly but persistently rounding off sharp corners.

.20

16.80 **Stop 9.** Park on shoulder.
On both sides of the road but more prominently on the left, a small red-brown dike slices through the Pen Formation. Also note the dull brown "baked zone" radiating away from the **dike,** half way up the hill. The baked zone formed when the hot, molten rock cut through the Pen Formation, literally cooking the sedimentary rocks it contacted. When **magma** is hot enough, sedimentary rock can actually be metamorphosed. In this case, the shale transformed into a **hornfels**.

You also see a number of small scale faults and fractures that carved through the Pen Formation. These faults provide

access to groundwater, facilitating the chemical **weathering** of the rock. For example, note the orange and brown stained veneer on the surfaces of the fractures. These secondary deposits were left by water as it seeped through the rock.

.40

17.20 **Slow down area.** Hot Springs Turnoff (stay on main road)
This road leads to one of several hot springs found in the West Texas area and along the Rio Grande. Although accessible at low water levels, the Langford Hot Springs can be submerged when river levels are running high.

All the hot springs in this region are believed to be related to normal faults. These Basin and Range type faults formed between 18 and 23 million years ago (Dasch, 1969). The earth's crust was slowly pulled apart and permanently thinned by these faults. Today groundwater circulating deep in the earth becomes heated before it returns to the surface as hot springs. (Chesser and Estepp, 1986).

.40

17.60 **Slow down area.**
If you look at the Boquillas Formation, you will see that it appears to be tilted or **dipping** in different directions. These variable **dips** were caused by the same normal faults that helped to create the hot springs. When the earth's crust was stretched by **faulting,** large blocks of rock pulled away from each other, dipping in different directions as they separated.

*Boquillas Formation,
mile 16.60.*

Dike, mile 16.80.

.60

18.20 **Stop 10.** Park on shoulder.
Look for an **alluvial fan** at this point. Most drainages that feed into this **alluvium** originate in the surrounding hills, composed of **Cretaceous**-age **sedimentary** rock.

.70

18.90 **Stop 11.** Park on pullout just before reaching the tunnel.
You are now driving past outcrops of the Santa Elena **Limestone,** a more massive layer than the Boquillas Limestone you saw at Stop 7. The Santa Elena Limestone is a solid bed of limestone while the Boquillas contains alternating layers of limestone and **shale.** Why are these two Cretaceous Period sedimentary rocks so different?

Since there are insignificant amounts of sands, silts, and **clays** present in the Santa Elena, most geologists believe that it formed some distance from shore, past the point where the sands and silts settle out of the water column. The Boquillas Formation has marine limestones and fossils present, so it undoubtedly formed in the Cretaceous seas also. However, the numerous shale layers suggest that the Boquillas Formation formed nearer the ancient shoreline than did the Santa Elena Formation.

Both the Santa Elena and Boquillas Formations are found in the same places throughout the park, yet apparently they tell us something different about the Cretaceous shoreline. Or did intense **faulting** perhaps thrust the Boquillas on top of the Santa Elena? Actually, these rocks record the migration of sea level with time. The blocky limestones of the Santa Elena formed strictly in a marine environment. As the ocean receded, terrigenous rocks dominated. This change in sea level, called a **regression,** is recorded in the Cretaceous rocks of Big Bend: from Santa Elena Limestone to Boquillas **flagstone** to Aguja and Javelina **clastic** deposits.

.05

18.95
The tunnel cuts through the Santa Elena Formation.

.35

19.30 **Slow down area.**
Look for dissected **alluvial fans** to your left. Behind them rise the commanding cliffs of the Santa Elena **Limestone.**

.40

19.70 **Turn left on the road to Boquillas Canyon and reset mileage to zero.**
0.00 Boquillas Canyon turn.

1.40

1.40 **Slow down area,** road on the right leads to the Boquillas crossing.
Several small caves in the cliff faces of the Santa Elena Limestone (left) formed through the combined forces of water and gravity. Water flowing between layers of rock slowly dissolved the limestone forming large hollows. As this undercutting continued, a cave began to evolve. The formation of the caves was enhanced as unsupported "roof" rocks collapsed, a

Panther Junction to Boquillas Canyon

process that continues today.

.30

1.70 Passing road to the Barker Lodge, presently used to house research scientists.

1.10

2.80 **Stop 12.** Turn to the right onto the paved spur road and drive to the Rio Grande and Boquillas Canyon overlook.
Look for large sand banks deposited by the Rio Grande as it ebbs and floods and changes its course. These **unlithified sediments** are readily reworked. Fickle winds scour and sort river sediments, removing fine to medium grained particles, and leaving behind sand. In this case, both water and wind have worked together to create the sand banks but the wind has been the dominate force in shaping the final deposit.

To the southwest, you can see the village of Boquillas, in the State of Coahuila, Mexico.

1.20

4.00 Marufo Vega Trail parking area. A short walk along the first half mile of the trail will lead you to the remains of a tramway tower. A six mile aerial tramway carrying zinc, silver, and lead ore from a mine in Mexico operated in this area from 1909 to 1919.

.70

4.70 Old ore tramway (circa 1910). An ore bucket is on the right.

.20

4.90 **Stop 13.** Parking lot at the head of Boquillas Canyon
Although this roadlog ends at the parking lot, you may choose to take the 3/4 mile trail to a giant canyon lined with huge blocks of Santa Elena **Limestone.** After climbing a small hill, the trail drops to the edge of the river before leading to the mouth of Boquillas Canyon.

The **Cretaceous** rocks observed today record the **regression** of sea level and the change from marine sedimentary units to **terrigenous** limestones . Although the process took millions of years, the change is well documented in the rocks of Big Bend. The surrounding cliffs serve as towering reminders of the marine heritage of the Big Bend country.

Panther Junction to Chisos Basin

Chisos Basin.

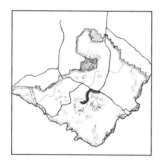

Panther Junction to Chisos Basin

Basin Junction to the Chisos Basin
(Suggested travel time: morning hours)
6.25 miles one way

The Chisos Basin Turnoff is located 3.15 miles west of Panther Junction Park Headquarters. The short drive from the turnoff will take you from the warm mid-elevations of the desert to the relatively cool volcanic highlands of the Chisos Mountains.

Mileage Reading
0.00 Chisos Basin Turnoff (after turning onto the Chisos Basin Road set your odometer to zero at the zero mile post).

.15

0.15 **Stop 1** – Park on pullout at the "Steep Grades/Winding Road" sign.
You are about to enter the high Chisos Mountains. Composed primarily of **igneous** rocks, these rugged mountains record the park's most violent period of geologic history. All **extrusive** rocks (**tuffs, ash,** and **lava flows**) in this area erupted from the Sierra Quemada and Pine Canyon Volcanoes between 35 and 32 million years ago. They erupted large amounts of volcanic material before collapsing into **calderas**.

Before their collapse the volcanoes were prominent peaks much higher than the highest mountains seen here today. However, since the volcanoes collapsed and formed calderas, much of the evidence for their precise position has been masked by more than 30 million years of **erosion**. The large amounts of ash and lava remaining tell geologists that the calderas once existed. Through careful studies, scientists have located the approximate position of both calderas. The Sierra Quemada Caldera is thought to have been in the southern foothills region of the Chisos Mountains while the Pine Canyon Caldera is thought to have been on the southeast side of the Chisos. Before collapsing, the Sierra Quemada Volcano erupted many of the sub-elements of the Chisos Formation, including the Tule Mountain **Trachyandesite,** Mule Ear Spring Tuff, Bee Mountain **Basalt,** Ash Spring Basalt and several unnamed flows and tuffs. On the other hand, all the rocks of the South Rim Formation, including the Burro Mesa **Rhyolite,** Lost Mine **Member,** Wasp Spring Member and other unnamed lava and ash flows can be traced to the Pine Canyon Volcano.

Throughout the park, the Chisos Formation rocks are found below the South Rim rocks. They are never found interlayered with one another. For this reason, geologists believe that the Sierra Quemada Volcano finished erupting and collapsed before the Pine Canyon Volcano became active.

*Pulliam Ridge,
mile .15.*

*Pinnacles on Pulliam
Ridge.*

The Chisos Mountains also contain many examples of intrusive igneous rocks. For example, the high mountain on the horizon to the right, Pulliam Ridge, is a **rhyolite intrusion**. It is one of the highest points in the park. However, its transformation from molten **magma** to solid rock occurred entirely beneath the Earth's surface. Covered at one time by hundreds of feet of **lava** and ash, the peak has come into view only through the slow and persistent process of erosion stripping away the overlying rocks.

Erosion has also revealed many smaller intrusions. For example, on the far right the low, rolling, red-colored hill is part of the Government Spring **Laccolith**. Although it also formed beneath the surface, it is compositionally a **syenite**, not a rhyolite as is Pulliam Ridge. In fact, these intrusions can be chemically quite diverse. However, as intrusions they all solidified beneath the Earth's crust and subsequently have been exposed by erosion.

.65

0.80 **Slow down area.**
The ridge to the immediate right of the road is a composite of Chisos Formation tuffs and two **ring dikes**. The dikes, which are more resistant to erosion than the tuffs, serve to hold up the ridge by slowing the onslaught of erosion.

1.40

2.20 **Stop 2** – Park on pullout at the Mountain Lion Country sign.
To the right lies a large accumulation of rubble exposed at the base of Pulliam Peak. The rubble is referred to as a **talus**

Panther Junction to Chisos Basin

deposit or talus slope. Talus deposits form when pieces of rock break off cliffs and are transported downslope by gravity. Pulliam Peak is etched by many **joints** and fractures. These features make it easier for large blocks of rock to be chiseled from the cliff face.

Although both talus and **alluvial** deposits form through erosion, there is an important distinction. In forming talus slopes, water breaks down the outcrop but gravity transports the rock fragments down the slope. In contrast, **alluvial fan** material is both broken down and moved by water.

Talus deposit, mile .15.

1.40

3.60 **Slow down area.**
Look for erosional pinnacles forming on the south side of Pulliam Peak.

.55

4.15 **Stop 3** – Park on pullout at the Green Gulch interpretive exhibit. Pulliam Ridge on the right.
The flat-topped, box-shaped mountain directly ahead to the south is Casa Grande literally translated from the Spanish as Big House. Home to peregrine falcons, Casa Grande is composed of volcanic rocks from both the Chisos and South Rim Formations. Lost Mine Peak, located to the southeast, is the result primarily of ash flows that erupted from the Pine Canyon Volcano.

Quite common throughout Big Bend, the black stains on the face of Pulliam Ridge (on the right) formed after water evaporated and deposited manganese oxide on the rock surfaces. The sentinel-like pinnacles are slowly disintegrating as erosion takes its toll on Pulliam Ridge.

Manganese oxide deposits, mile 4.15.

Casa Grande.

*Casa Grande air fall
tuffs.*

1.00

5.15 Lost Mine Trailhead.
Try to make time for this 4.8 mile round-trip hike. An informative trail folder is available at the trailhead.

.15

5.30 **Stop 4** — Park on pullout.
Here you have a splendid view of Casa Grande on the left. Casa Grande, composed of deposits from both the Sierra Quemada and Pine Canyon Volcanoes provides a good perspective on how the resistance to erosion influences the evolution of the landscape. For instance, the massive ash flow units capping Casa Grande are part of the South Rim Formation. Very slow to erode, they form the solid cliffs of the mountain. In contrast, the lower portions of Casa Grande are composed of the thinly-layered lava flows and **air fall tuffs** of the Chisos Formation. These softer rocks erode more easily, forming gentle slopes. Several areas in the park, including Goat Mountain and Cerro Castellan, display the same rock series: the cliff-forming South Rim Formation on top of the slope-forming Chisos Formation.

.40

5.70 **Stop 5** — Park on pullout.
Below spreads a panorama of intrusive formations — from right to left: Pulliam Ridge, Vernon Bailey Peak, Amon Carter Peak, and Ward Mountain — forming the northern, western, and southwestern rims of the Basin. All these rocks solidified within the Earth, covered by layer upon layer of volcanic rocks of the Chisos and

26

South Rim Formations. Look for The Window, a V-shaped notch that separates Vernon Bailey and Amon Carter Peaks. Water draining through the Basin removed the overlying extrusive rocks and carved The Window. Oak Creek now occupies this drainage path. The interface between the extrusive and intrusive rocks is probably nearby because streams and creeks frequently flow along this **contact** zone. Since contact zone rocks erode more easily than **monolithic** rock, they provide a less resistant pathway for water.

A dark **volcaniclastic** deposit of the Chisos Formation is exposed on the left side of the road. The well-rounded pebbles and layered appearance of this deposit are testimony to the impact of stream activity. When initially deposited, this unit contained numerous sharp rock fragments. However, flowing water picked up the jagged pieces, sorted the particles by size, rounded off sharp edges and then redeposited them. In fact, the entire Basin has been cut by water. Where is all that water today? Remember, that the climate is not static through time. Geologists believe that the **paleoclimate** here during **Tertiary** times was much more humid. Abundant rainfall and perennial streams, responsible for starting erosion in the Basin, were dominant forces then.

.35

6.05 Campground Entrance. Stay to your left passing the turn off to the campground.

.20

6.25 **Stop 6.** Chisos Basin Parking Lot.

From the parking lot, Casa Grande Peak towers above the Chisos Mountains Lodge and the rim-forming peaks of the Basin: Toll Mountain, with its numerous pinnacles and Emory Peak, the park's highest point, are all composed of extrusive igneous rocks. They form the south and southeast Basin rim. Pulliam Ridge, Vernon Bailey Peak, Amon Carter Peak, and Ward Mountain, all intrusives, form the north, west, and southwest Basin rim.

Portions of a ring dike, exposed both behind the restaurant and as a promontory near the center of the Basin, once cut across the Basin. Standing in bold relief because of its resistance to erosion, the dike contains two minerals: white-colored **feldspar** and clear glassy quartz. Blocks of the ring dike rock, scattered about as boulders, are easily identified by the presence of these two minerals.

Panther Junction to West Entrance

Maverick Badlands.

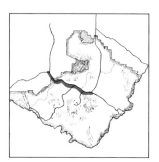

Panther Junction to West Entrance

Panther Junction Park Headquarters to Study Butte
(Suggested travel time: morning hours)
22.60 miles one way

This trip reveals both **igneous** and **sedimentary** rocks. Numerous roadcuts illustrate rock types and evidence of geologic processes that are more pieces to the puzzle of Big Bend's geologic past. Drive carefully on this well-traveled route, especially when leaving and entering the traffic flow.

Mileage Reading
0.00 Panther Junction Park Headquarters at stop sign.

.20

.20 **Slow down area,** service station
Lone Mountain (on the right), consisting of sedimentary units of the **Aguja Formation** in the lower slopes and a capping ring dike layer, stands to the north of the road.

1.80

2.00 **Slow down area.**
You are driving on alluvial material that originated in the Chisos Mountains; the thick alluvial accumulations show the power of erosion working through time. Left of the road, the layered hills are composed of Chisos Formation tuffs and lava flows.

.90

2.90 **Stop 1** – Park on pullout.
Southwest of the road (left) rise the igneous rocks comprising the Chisos Mountains. The promontories constructed of intrusive rocks, such as Pulliam Peak, and extrusive rocks, such as Casa Grande, create the highest topographic relief in the park.

.20

3.10 More alluvial deposits are exposed here.

.05

3.15 Intersection of the main road and Chisos Basin road, stay on main park road.

.40

3.55 **Stop 2** – Park on shoulder just past the Grapevine Hills Road.

The Grapevine Hills rise to the north-northeast on the right. These hills formed within the Earth when magma was trapped and solidified at depth instead of erupting at the surface. These **syenite** intrusive rocks have been uncovered by erosion only recently, geologically speaking. The rocks in the immediate area are part of another intrusion, the Government Spring Laccolith, which is also a syenite.

On the left side of the road you can see and feel the impact of **weathering** and erosion on the Government Spring Laccolith. The rounded crumbly masses of orange stained rock are examples of **spheroidal weathering**. Spheroidal weathering occurs here for two reasons. First, the laccolith is fractured, broken into tabular and angular bodies that provide avenues for water to filter into the blocky rock mass. Second, chemical weathering more intensely attacks the edges of these blocks, rapidly rounding the sharp corners. The staining, the result of streaks and patches of secondary iron oxide deposits, also owes its existence to water. The highly altered outcrop represents the end-product of these processes.

.65
4.20 – 4.40 **Slow down area.**
The undulating ridge on the left hand side of the road is the Government Spring Laccolith.

.80

5.00 **Slow down area.**

The road passes through more alluvial material derived from the Chisos Mountains.

1.20

6.20 **Stop 3** – Park on shoulder at the Paint Gap Hills Road.

To the left the Chisos Mountains dominate the skyline. These rugged mountains are composed of lava and ash deposits from the extrusive Chisos and South Rim Formations and massive, rounded intrusive outcrops. Two laccoliths are also visible from this vantage. On the right you can see Paint Gap Hills to the northeast and Croton Peak to the northwest.

The flat-topped mountain on the horizon near the western slope of Paint Gap Hills is Santiago Peak. It is yet another Tertiary-age intrusion. Located outside the park boundary, Santiago Peak has a colorful history. In the early 1900s an enterprising, if not totally honest, entrepreneur staked out a city on the top of Santiago Peak. Armed with scenic snapshots taken from the summit, the would-be developer journeyed east to sell plots of his mountain-top community of Progress City. In his sales pitch he failed to mention that the property lacked water and electric services and that no roads readily climbed to the crest of the mountain. He successfully sold several plots before the land scam was uncovered. Now, Progress City exists only in the memory of some oldtimers and in blueprints still on file in the Brewster County Courthouse in Alpine, Texas.

1.40

7.60 **Slow down area.**

To the left, alluvial fans make up the lower slopes of the Chisos Mountains and grade into the sloping **pediment** surface you are driving on.

.90

8.50 **Slow down area**.
The road cuts through a major alluvial fan as you descend Todd Hill.

.50

Santiago Peak.

9.00 **Stop 4** – Park on shoulder.
The dark rock forming a small hill on the right is a **sill,** another kind of igneous intrusion. Unlike dikes that cut through existing horizontal rock layers, sills form when magma squeezes between rock layers. Chemically the rock creating the sill is **basanite,** meaning that it contains even less **silica** than a basalt does. This rock, 44.5 million years old, is one of the oldest igneous rocks discovered and dated thus far in Big Bend.

.60

9.60 **Slow down area**.
The dark-colored rock scattered on the ground here comes from the basanite sill. When rocks become detached from the main outcrop and are strewn on the ground, geologists call them **"float."** Float, a general term, can refer to sedimentary, metamorphic or igneous rock fragments.

Basanite sill, mile 9.00.

.30

9.90 **Stop 5** – Park on shoulder at the Croton Springs Road.
Cross the road and walk about 0.2 mile to the top of the hill. Looking down on the

stream bed you can see that the recent veneer of **alluvium** lies directly on the top of the Aguja Formation. We know that Tertiary Period rocks should be here, sandwiched between the **Cretaceous** Aguja Formation and the recent alluvium, yet they are notably absent. Evidently, before the alluvium was deposited erosion worked to strip away the Tertiary-age units that were once here.

To the left, the Chisos Mountains tower above the desert floor. The tan and light-pink colored pillars, best seen in afternoon light, standing on the flanks of the mountains are tuffs and ash flows of the South Rim Formation. Here the bold contact between the South Rim rocks and the dark brown intrusive mass of Pulliam Peak is evident. Through **radiometric dating,** ages of many of the Chisos Mountains intrusions have been determined to be about 32 million years. The age of Pulliam Peak itself remains undetermined. Using **relative age** criteria, in this case one deposit cutting through another, you can be certain that Pulliam Peak is younger than the flows it slices through.

.60

10.50 **Stop 6** – Park on shoulder.
To the left of the road are low-lying knobs perched slightly above the desert floor. These are **sandstone** beds of the Aguja Formation, the less resistant **shales** and **siltstones** having already been carried away. Walk among these knobs and look for their interesting sedimentary features: ripple marks and cross bedding. In addition, some sandstone layers contain abundant marine fossils. The presence of these sedimentary features and fossils suggests that this part of the Aguja Formation developed in a beach-like **near-shore** setting. Imagine this outcrop during the Cretaceous: the ripples forming as warm waves washed across the beach, removing wastes and bringing nutrients to the clams and other organisms living in the sediments.

.60

11.10 **Stop 7** – Park on shoulder.
Sandstones of the Aguja Formation are clearly exposed on both sides of the road. The light gray sandstones display a variety of secondary weathering. For instance, the orange-brown concentric rings of color, called **liesegang banding,** result from the deposition of iron oxide minerals by water as it passes through the sandstone. Numerous fractures provide avenues for water to migrate into the rock layers, accelerating erosion and chemical weathering. The western portion of the outcrop reveals an area of crumbly yellow-white sandstone. This coloration and texture, produced by **hydrothermal** alteration, literally the action of hot water, occurred when scalding groundwater assaulted the original sandstone, destroying primary minerals and leaving in its wake the deposit you see today.

.60

11.70 **Stop 8** – Park on shoulder just before reaching the bridge.
To the left stands a flat-topped hill. A sill, capping the underlying sandstones and siltstones of the Aguja Formation, has slowed erosion.

The dark basanite rock of Slickrock Mountain can be seen to the far right. The

fault scarp of the Burro Mesa fault is directly ahead forming the skyline. Also ahead, a pyramid-shaped hill capped by a sandstone identifies the Aguja Formation.

1.10

12.80 **Slow down area**.
The road continues to be bracketed by outcrops of the Aguja Formation. The more resistant sandstones have better survived the onslaught of erosion than the much softer surrounding shale units.

.30

Liesegang banding, mile 11.10.

13.10
Intersection of main road and Ross Maxwell Scenic Drive. Stay on main road.

.40

13.50 **Slow down area**.
The stream crossing of Cottonwood Creek exposes coarse **conglomerate** beds interbedded with layers of sand and silt, a good view of the variable nature of recent alluvium. These alluvial deposits do not form by single, isolated events. Rather, several small to large scale episodes of deposition are recorded. The next major rainfall will likely change the face of this outcrop: water will cut new channels and add new rock, gravel and sand to this evolving outcrop.

Recent alluvium, mile 13.60.

1.50

15.00 **Stop 9** — Park on pullout.
At this point, the road parallels the trace of the Burro Mesa Fault, defined by the streambed, below and to the right. Streams

Tule Mountain.

*Collapsed volcanic
vent, mile 16.70.*

frequently mark the position of faults; the movement along faults grinds and weakens the rocks, creating the path of least resistance for water. We know that the fault cuts through here because the Tertiary-age igneous rocks of the Chisos Formation abuts the Cretaceous sedimentary units of the Aguja and Pen Formations.

1.70

16.70 **Stop 10** – Park on shoulder.
To the left the dark capped ridge is a small collapsed volcanic vent that was first identified by Ross Maxwell. The lava flows probably gained this orientation when the column of magma feeding the central intrusion was depleted, causing the unsupported intrusion and overlying lavas to collapse.

.80

17.50 **Slow down area**.
To the left Burro Mesa is composed of a number of volcanic flow units including the Burro Mesa Rhyolite and Wasp Springs member of the South Rim Formation and the Tule Mountain Trachyandesite and several air fall tuffs of the Chisos Formation. The Chisos Mountains stand behind Burro Mesa and Tule Mountain lies to the right of Burro Mesa. The large notch cutting through the distant cliff face to the west southwest is Santa Elena Canyon. Maverick Mountain, another intrusive rock, is exposed to the west-northwest as the prominent, well-rounded hill.

3.70

21.20 **Stop 11** – Park on shoulder and

walk to the canyon on the right.

The striking red, purple, and green **mudstones** of the Aguja Formation owe their coloration to the destruction of primary minerals and secondary deposition of iron and manganese oxides.

Many of the Tertiary-age igneous mountains can be seen from this vantage. In the far distance to the northeast, are intrusive rocks of the Christmas Mountains, which have been mined for fluorite, a calcium fluoride mineral. Immediately in front of these are the little Christmas Mountains, still another series of exposed intrusions. To the northeast locate Dogie Mountain, composed of tuffs, lavas and Cretaceous sedimentary units. Due north, on your immediate right, is Maverick Mountain, a rhyolite (**silica-rich**) intrusion. Maverick Mountain appears to have rock layers peeling off its sides. This is a fairly common feature, termed **exfoliation**, displayed by some igneous rocks. Almost due south is Tule Mountain.

.80

22.00 **Slow down area.**
The brightly colored Aguja Formation mudstones form the rounded hills on the canyon floor. Two prominent dark colored dikes punch through the mudstone on the left.

.30

22.30 **Slow down area.**
At this point, on the left, a dike intersects the road.

.10

22.40 **Stop 12** – Park on shoulder.
On the east (right) side of the road a dike is helping to preserve the Cretaceous-age Pen Formation, creating a knife-like promontory. Take a short walk to this point and look closely at the outcrop. When the molten magma entered the Pen Formation it spread out following several different pathways. As it solidified the "fingers" of rock forming the dike acted as reinforcing rods placed in the mudstones, slowing down the process of erosion.

Also note the contact between the dike and sedimentary rocks. A breccia zone, contact breccia, consisting of a dike holding rock fragments of the Pen Formation marks the magma's path as it ripped up sedimentary rocks in its way, incorporating them in the surface of the solidifying dike. The abundant crystals filling voids throughout the rock and scattered about on the desert floor are secondary deposits of **calcite** and **gypsum**.

.20

22.60 **Exit Big Bend National Park.**
On this route you've observed how ancient seas, explosive volcanoes, **faulting,** and erosion have worked together to shape the landscape, creating features like the small promontory at the previous stop, the Burro Mesa fault scarp, and the magnificent Chisos Mountains. No one process could have produced the Big Bend country. The region's splendor is a legacy of its rich and diverse geologic past.

Mule Ears.

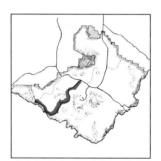

Ross Maxwell to Santa Elena Canyon

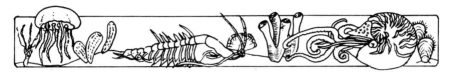

Ross Maxwell Scenic Drive

(Suggested travel time: morning hours)

32 miles one way

Traversing some of the most intriguing outcrops of **igneous** rocks to be found in Big Bend, this drive ends at the massive, faulted **limestone** cliffs of Santa Elena Canyon. Although it is only 32 miles long, expect your explorations to take the better part of a day, particularly if you choose to take the suggested hikes at Burro Mesa Pouroff and Tuff Canyon.

This roadlog begins at the turnoff to the Ross Maxwell Scenic Drive from the main park road, 13.1 miles west of Panther Junction Park Headquarters. Re-set your trip odometer at the start of the drive.

Mileage Reading

0.00 Start of Ross Maxwell Scenic Drive.

.50

.50 **Stop 1** – Park on shoulder just past the dry wash.

The paved road passes over **Cretaceous**-age sedimentary rocks that cover the desert floor and butt against the Chisos Formation igneous rocks exposed in the Burro Mesa fault to the right. The juxtaposition of the Cretaceous and **Tertiary** rocks is conclusive evidence that a fault sliced through the rocks, disrupting the normal stratigraphic sequence. Even though they lie beneath the adjacent igneous flows, the Cretaceous rocks are part of the upthrown fault block. Initially, when **faulting** thrust it upward, the block contained thick deposits of Tertiary-age sediments and **lava flows** in addition to the Cretaceous rocks. Erosion stripped away the younger rocks, tearing down the upthrown block and exposing the Cretaceous rocks.

The Cretaceous-age Aguja sediments crop out at road level. To the left rises a small hill, its base composed of tan to gray Aguja sediments and covered by dark brown **Javelina Formation** sediments. Recent **alluvial** deposits, formed from erosion of the Chisos Mountains, cap the hill. To the left, Pulliam Ridge and Ward Mountain, Chisos Basin intrusives, form the major part of the Chisos Mountains skyline.

.45

.95 **Stop 2** – Park on pullout on the left.

Straight ahead stand the Chisos Mountains, including from left to right Vernon Bailey Peak, The Window, and Ward Mountain. To the right of Ward Mountain, dark flows of the Ash Spring **Basalt** form the cliff resting on the layered Chisos Formation **tuffs**.

On the left look for the small isolated knob of Javelina Formation **sandstone** capped by a **sill**. Acting as a hard resistant cover, this sill protects the sandstone and slows **erosion**. Many such knobs are momentarily preserved throughout the park, but in time the unrelenting attack of erosion will eventually level them.

1.05

2.00 **Stop 3** – Park on pullout on the left.
An excellent vista of the volcanic highlands with Casa Grande apparently perched at the throat of The Window unfolds on the left. Casa Grande is made up of **extrusive** volcanics, in contrast to the intrusive volcanics that frame The Window. Sedimentary units – **shales, siltstones,** and sandstones – of the Cretaceous- age Javelina Formation, appear in the immediate foreground. Although the nearby Chisos Mountains served as a focal point for explosive volcanic activity, no igneous rocks cover these older sediments. Certainly hot lava and ash once poured over this entire area, inundating the Cretaceous units. However, geologists believe that erosion slowly removed younger rock layers, finally uncovering the Cretaceous rocks visible today.

On the right side of the road, layered tuffs and flows of the Chisos Formation appear. The alternating sequence of units, characteristic of the Chisos Formation, appears time and again throughout the park.

1.00

3.00 **Stop 4** – Park on pulloff on the left.

On the left, look at the Vernon Bailey Pea **intrusion** punching through the Chiso Formation rocks. Although Vernon Baile Peak appears massive and indestructibl several small canyons cut by intermitten streams deeply etch its face (best seen i afternoon light). These canyons ar reminders that erosion remains activ today. Left unchecked by the onset of new stage of mountain building, erosio will one day raze the entire Chisos Moun tain complex, including this mighty peak.

In the foreground, the colorful sed mentary rocks of the Javelina Formatio continue, here covered with a thin venee of alluvial rubble.

To the right and especially to the nort behind you, deposits of the Chisos Forma tion appear, good examples of the **differ ential** erosion process. The less resistan tuffs erode more quickly, forming th slopes; the relatively harder lava flow erode more slowly, forming cliffs.

.40

3.40 **Slow down area**, Sam Nail Ranc Exhibit on the right.
The several prominent, knife-like ridge piercing the desert floor on the left forme when craggy **dikes** were uncovered by er sion. Unlike **ring dikes** (see Persimmo Gap and Basin roadlogs) these dikes ar not associated with **caldera** formatio Among the youngest igneous rocks in th park (17-20 million years old), these dike formed during the **Basin and Rang faulting**.

.70

4.10 **Stop 5** – Park on pullout on th

left.
This exhibit depicts the history of the dikes. Remember that it is only through erosion that we see these dikes at all.

On the right side of the road large boulders loosened by erosion from the surrounding formations litter the slopes.

1.40

5.50 Stop 6 – Park on pullout on the left.
On the left side of the road, near the top of the thin-bedded Chisos Formation tuffs, lies a dark, cliff- forming unit of the Bee Mountain Basalt. This same rock type appears on the more massive southern hill but at a noticeably lower elevation. A normal fault displaced these rocks, lifting the tuffs and dropping the southern block. As with all normal faults in Big Bend, this fault occurred 17-20 million years ago, during Basin and Range times.

Here the Bee Mountain Basalt also forms the major cliffs exposed to the left, midway upslope. This basalt flow traverses the mountain face, following an apparent zig-zag course. The flows were displaced when the earth's crust pulled apart in response to normal faulting.

1.40

6.90 Stop 7 – Park on pullout.
In this roadcut watch for a dike, approximately 16 feet (five meters) across, cutting through the gray **volcaniclastic** unit, best seen on the left. Look carefully at the dike and identify the **phenocryst** of alkali **feldspar** (white) and quartz (clear). These are **silica-rich** minerals, indicating that this dike is **rhyolitic** in composition. The white

coating on the dike's surface is **caliche,** a secondary deposit that frequently forms in arid environments. Follow the dike as it extends towards the Chisos Mountains. Note that it cuts through the lava beds and is therefore younger material.

.50

7.40 Stop 8 – Park on pullout.
Erosion is chiseling a canyon on the left side of the road. Across the canyon to the left, a dike embedded in and apparently displacing the Bee Mountain Basalt occurs. As frequently happens, pre-existing fractures in rocks, a fault in this case, offer an easy course for ascending **magmas** to follow. Rather than slicing pathways directly through solid rock, magmas rise through these fractures.

.70

8.10 Stop 9 – Park on pullout at the Blue Creek Ranch Overlook **on the left**. Take the short walk from the parking area to the overlook.
Several Bee Mountain Basalt lava flows are exposed in the walls of Blue Creek Canyon. A gray tuff layer separates these flows, telling geologists that volcanic activity was cyclical. Evidently, the Sierra Quemada Volcano erupted thick basaltic lava flows, then filled the air with ash. After the ash settled, another basaltic lava spilled down the flanks of the volcano and covered the earlier flows. The rocks in the canyon wall record this series of events and indicate a very dynamic geologic story.

Burro Mesa rises on the right hand side of the road. Capped by its namesake,

*Santa Elena Canyon
from Sotol Vista.*

*Chisos Formation,
mile 8.30.*

the Burro Mesa Rhyolite, it consists of both Chisos and South Rim Formation units. Although younger than the Bee Mountain Basalt exposed in the canyon, the South Rim rocks found on Burro Mesa are topographically lower. One would expect the South Rim Formation rocks to be above the older Chisos Formation units. The two formations are out of sequence because normal faulting dropped the western block of rocks down relative to the ones you stand on here.

To the south, across Blue Creek Canyon, flows of both the Chisos and South Rim formations display the expected stratigraphic sequence. The lowest cliff- forming unit, the Bee Mountain Basalt, is Chisos Formation while the uppermost cliff-forming unit, the Lost Mine Rhyolite, is of the South Rim Formation. The base of the Lost Mine Rhyolite cliff marks the contact beneath the formations.

.20

8.30 **Stop 10** – Turn left at Sotol Vista and drive to the overlook. Get out of your vehicle at the parking area and walk to the overlook exhibit.
On the western horizon gapes the mouth of Santa Elena Canyon. Here the Rio Grande carved through more than 1600 feet (500 meters) of Cretaceous rocks to create the majestic canyon. The green blanket of vegetation downstream from the canyon tracks the course of the Rio Grande as it cuts across the desert floor separating the United States and Mexico.

Looking back toward the previous stop, you can see the now familiar rocks of both the red-colored Chisos and the gray South Rim formations, all products of two powerful volcanoes that dominated the

40

region during the Tertiary Age. Locate the fault, cutting north to south, that offsets these rocks. Chisos Formation rocks lie on the east side of the fault; South Rim Formation rocks lie to the west. To the northwest is Burro Mesa, the site of the next stop.

The road leaves Sotol Vista, to the west, travelling downward through mountainous accumulations of recent alluvial material. Intermittent stream activity carried these rock fragments from their source, finally leaving them on the downdropped block of the normal fault.

Restart mileage at the junction of Ross Maxwell Scenic Drive.

9.30 Slow down area, caution, sharp turn.
Although the deposit on the right contains a variety of rock shapes and sizes, virtually all the fragments here originated in the Chisos Mountains. Rounded pieces of the Bee Mountain Basalt and Ash Spring Basalt abound. As you descend the mountain notice the crude layering that has developed in the **alluvium** on both sides of the road. It indicates that the alluvial material was deposited intermittently. Each layer records a different stage in the history of this **alluvial fan.**

2.30

11.60 Stop 11 – Turn right at the entrance to Burro Mesa Pouroff and park on shoulder.
To the right, the talus slope portion of Burro Mesa displays a bold contact zone identified by a tan layer of South Rim ash. Above the zone lies the South Rim Formation; below the zone lies the Chisos Forma-

tion. This impressive mesa evolved in stages. Eruptions, first from the Sierra Quemada Volcano followed by eruptions from the Pine Canyon Volcano, contributed lava and ash during the cataclysmic mid-Tertiary period. Since then, **weathering** and erosion have cut into the rock, sculpting the landform you see today.

To the north, the characteristic light gray to white tuffs of the Chisos Formation crop out. These tuffs are ash "falls", not ash flows. The thinly- bedded ash layers formed when ash cooled and settled out of the atmosphere, blanketing the land. Therefore, they erode more quickly than massive ash flows and tend to form slopes rather than cliffs. In the foreground on the right side of the hill an Ash Spring Basalt lava flow is exposed. Most of the hill, though, is made up of intrusive materials. The prominent **columnar jointing** indicates that the intrusion cooled near the surface.

Drive to the end of the road and park.

1.70

13.30 Stop 12 – Stop at the end of the road at the trailhead to Burro Mesa Pouroff.
A short (one mile roundtrip) trail leads to the pouroff. Along the trail watch for abundant volcaniclastic deposits containing numerous large cobbles and boulders. As you face the canyon the cliff to your left is composed of South Rim Formation units. Closer examination of this formation reveals slopes composed of Chisos Formation tuffs resting on top of dark colored Bee Mountain Basalt. The dark rock capping the cliff is Burro Mesa Rhyolite, probably a highly welded ash flow. The lighter

*Wasp Spring Flow
Breccia, mile 13.30.*

*Many of the rocks on
the ground have a
black patina which is
typical of desert
varnish, mile 13.90.*

colored bed just below is an ash flow deposit called Wasp Spring Flow Breccia.

Below the Wasp Spring Flow Breccia is a conglomerate composed of well rounded cobbles and boulders of many different intrusive and extrusive igneous rocks embedded in an ash matrix. As you follow the trail to the right in the canyon, the conglomerate beds crop out along the sides of the stream bed. Keep in mind that these rocks came from the Pine Canyon volcano. A similar valley fill can be seen on Goat Mountain.

Ash flows move either as a hot dense powdery mass that flows downslope, or, as a liquid slurry of ash and water that flows down the valley. In either case, they move at speeds of 60-80 miles per hour and are very destructive. The size of the boulders in the conglomerate indicates that swift currents were required to move them.

As you walk toward the pouroff note the large hollows in the Wasp Spring Flow Breccia. These hollows mark places from which suspended boulders have been displaced and sent crashing to the valley floor. At the trail's end you will see the stained, polished rocks of the pouroff. Although running water is absent most of the year these rocks have been eroded by intermittent water falls that develop during the summer rainy season.

Restart mileage at the junction of Ross Maxwell Scenic Drive

13.90 **Slow down area**.
The gray, tan, and red Chisos Formation tuffs line the roadway. Many of the rocks scattered about wear a black coating of manganese oxide stain. This staining, referred to as **desert varnish**, occurs com-

monly throughout the park.

.90

14.80 **Stop 13** – Park on pullout on your left. Get out of your vehicle and look back. The commanding height of Goat Mountain is impressive compared to the surrounding landscape, yet for much of its existence Goat Mountain was a canyon. How can you tell? The rock layers exposed in Goat Mountain do not run continuously across its face. Indeed, many rock layers show up on the right and left sides of the mountain but are missing in the center. Since ash and lava settle or flow uniformly, they tend to envelop an entire area. But this mountain reveals a more complex story. Streams cut through the once continuous layers of rock, creating channels. These channels then filled with lava and ash during volcanic eruptions, momentarily blocking the streams. Even now there is evidence of new canyons being cut. Unless volcanoes erupt again in Big Bend (most geologists think this is unlikely in the near geologic future) streams will continue to carve new and deeper channels into Goat Mountain.

.70

15.50 **Stop 14** – Turn left at the Mule Ears Turnoff and drive one-half mile to the trailhead.

Mule Ears, a prime example of a landform shaped by erosion, is composed of resistant Bee Mountain Basalt at its base overlaid by the Mule Ear Spring Tuff and finally capped by spire-like dikes. Although you may find it difficult to envision, the Mule Ear Spring Tuff was once continuous between the "ears." The highly fractured and jointed tuff accelerated erosion because it provided access to moisture. If erosion continues unchallenged by other natural processes, Mule Ears will eventually be leveled.

Restart mileage at the junction of Ross Maxwell Scenic Drive.

.85

16.35 **Slow down area**.
The road cuts through a layer of Alamo Creek Basalt, one of the oldest igneous units in the park. At the western end of the roadcut, look for the Alamo Creek Basalt lying on the brown, tan, and red sedimentary rocks of the Javelina Formation. Remember that the Javelina Formation is Cretaceous-age; the Alamo Creek is Tertiary-age. Early Tertiary-Age sediments, notably the Canoe and Hanold Hill formations, should be sandwiched between the basalts and Cretaceous rocks. Their absence indicates that a time gap, an **unconformity,** exists here.

2.40

18.75 **Slow down area**.
Directly ahead is Cerro Castellan. Like Casa Grande and Burro Mesa, Cerro Castellan is composed of igneous rocks from both the Sierra Quemada (Chisos Formation) and Pine Canyon (South Rim Formation) volcanoes. Although the volcanoes were centered several miles from this point, the igneous deposits here are incredibly thick. The massive accumulation of lava and ash emphasizes the fact that the two volcanoes spewed out tremendous amounts of rock material that engulfed the

*Fault cutting through
ash and basalt,
mile 19.80.*

Pink tuff, mile 20.20.

area between here and the Basin. Today only token remnants of these once vast deposits remain preserved in promontories like Goat Mountain and Cerro Castellan.

1.05

19.80 **Stop 15** – Park on pulloff at the Tuff Canyon Overlook.

Peering at the Chisos Formation tuffs exposed below in the walls of Tuff Canyon gives you a sense of the enormous amount of material erupted during the Tertiary period. Time after time the Sierra Quemada Volcano coughed ash into the atmosphere which settled, layer upon layer, onto the ground. The short hike into Tuff Canyon reveals ash layers similar to those observed earlier at Burro Mesa Pouroff. Off to the far right, a short walk to another overlook reveals a small fault at the upper end of the canyon. Here you can see a wall-like layer of basalt. Since the faulting cuts through layers of lava flows, tuff layers and **mudflows,** the faulting must have occurred after the volcanic activity.

.40

20.20 **Slow down area,** River Road junction.

The pink tuff material on the left, dissected by rainfall, is part of the Chisos Formation.

.45

20.65 **Slow down area**.

Erosion whittled a small "eye" or window into an outcrop of the South Rim Formation visible on the right. Further to the left, note the gray tuffs of the Wasp Spring Formation.

.45

21.10 **Stop 16** – Park on pullout on the left.

At this spot magma intruded into the Chisos Formation tuffs. Since no fault or fracture guided the development of this intrusion, it solidified in atypical forms. Observe, for example, part of the intrusion on the right side of the road that in both shape and texture resembles a fossilized tree. You may wish to cross the road and walk approximately 50 yards uphill to the intrusion.

The abundant white material in this area is airfall tuff, a deposit of loose ash that fell from the air after a volcano erupted. The volcanic ash is composed of tiny slivers or shards of glassy rock.

Cerro Castellan towers above you at 3,293 feet (1,003 meters). Note the three distinct layers of igneous rock. From top to bottom the named rock formations are: Burro Mesa Riebeckite Rhyolite, Wasp Spring Flow **Breccia,** and Bee Mountain Basalt.

*Cerro Castellan,
mile 21.10.*

1.40

22.50 Turnoff to the Castolon Historic Area on the left. Here you will find restrooms, a general store, and a ranger station.

.70

23.20 **Slow down area,** Cottonwood Campground.

The road travels along Tertiary to recent alluvial deposits comprising the Rio Grande floodplain. Farmers raised cotton and vegetables on this fertile land from the

*Intrusion resembling a
fossilized tree.*

Mouth of Santa Elena Canyon (1,500') compared to San Antonio's Tower of Americas (750').

Aguja Formation, mile .90.

1800s into the 1900s.

0.00 Restart mileage at the gate to zero.

.90

.90 **Stop 17** – Park on the far end of the pullout **on the left.**
Just ahead to the right, outcrops of the Cretaceous-age Aguja Formation, composed of interbedded sandstones and shales, tilt steeply because of the Terlingua Fault.
Below, the Rio Grande winds its way across the desert. Much of the water at this point comes from the Rio Conchos, a river originating in Mexico that joins the Rio Grande near Presidio, Texas.

.20

1.10 **Stop 18** – Park on pullout.
Off to the right and behind you, Cerro Castolon, Goat Mountain, Mule Ears, Burro Mesa, and the Chisos Mountains rise. Immense volumes of ash and lava erupted during the Tertiary periods and covered this entire landscape. Since then erosive forces have dissected the terrain, carving valleys and sculpting mountains. In fact, without erosion, this region would be relatively bland and featureless; a faulted plain of volcanic ash would stretch to the horizon.

2.20

3.30 **Stop 19** – Park on pullout on the left.
Across the Rio Grande running water has cut a stair-step pathway into the cliffs of the

Sierra Ponce in Chihuahua, Mexico. If the water had been permanent enough, another canyon, perhaps rivaling Santa Elena, might have developed.

3.50

6.80 **Stop 20** — Turn left at Santa Elena Canyon Overlook.
We can reconstruct the evolutionary history of the canyon beginning with the deposition of numerous layers of muds, silts and sands during the Cretaceous and early Cenozoic. Time and pressure transformed these soft sediments into sedimentary rocks. The lavas and ash deposits from the volcanoes active during the middle Cenozoic were deposited over these sedimentary rocks. Then, during the Basin and Range extension a normal fault (the Terlinqua Fault) formed where the cliffs now cross the Rio Grande at the entrance to Santa Elena Canyon. The fault block containing Santa Elena Canyon was uplifted relative to the block where the canyon overlook is now located. Later, when the Rio Grande reached the Big Bend area, it eroded Santa Elena Canyon as well as Mariscal and Boquillas canyons.

There are two principal theories about how the canyons formed. In the first theory, called the antecedent theory, the ancestral Rio Grande established its course prior to the Basin and Range faulting. As it slowly cut its channel deeper into the massive limestones the uplift of one fault block continued. The end result was a magnificent steep-walled canyon.

In the second theory, called the superimposed theory, the ancestral Rio Grande was located on the coastal plain east of the present Sierra del Carmen and the Santiago Mountains while the Basin and Range faulting was taking place. The closed basins formed by the faulting slowly filled with sediment eroded from the Chisos Mountains and from the upturned edges of the fault blocks. Each basin then overflowed into the next lower basin until finally a single large basin formed centered in northern Mexico. As the mountains rose during the Pliocene and as the Pleistocene began, precipitation increased. The basin then overflowed the Sierra del Carmen at a structurally low point and flowed into the ancestral Rio Grande on the coastal plain.

Today the Rio Grande erodes rapidly headward into the mountains. It erodes downward through the basin and is superimposed on the hard limestones. When the Rio Grande erodes headward, the major canyons in the park are cut: first, Boquillas Canyon, cut into the upturned edge of the fault block; second, Mariscal Canyon, cut into a Cretaceous-early Cenozoic anticline; and third, Santa Elena Canyon, cut into the upturned edge of a fault block (King, P.B., 1935).

Turn left to reach the Old Maverick Road. The Maverick Road will be on your right.

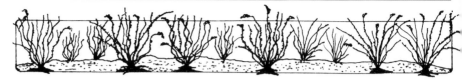

Ocotillo near Maverick.

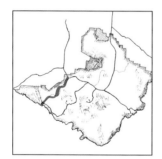

Maverick Road

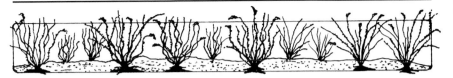

Maverick Road
(Suggested travel time: morning or late afternoon)
12.80 miles one way

This unimproved road provides access to some of the best examples of modern day processes affecting landscape development in the park. Beginning near the Santa Elena Canyon overlook, this road is often rather rough. Be sure to check road conditions, before beginning your trip, especially during rainy weather.

Mileage Reading
0.00 Beginning of road. Re-set your trip odometer.
The road winds past **sediments** of the **Cretaceous**-age **Aguja Formation**. Only a thin layer of the **rubbly alluvial** gravel covers the Aguja rocks; the volcanic rocks have long since been dislodged and removed by erosion.

.50

.50 **Stop 1** – Park on the right.
The valley to the north and west harbors Terlingua Creek. For most of the year Terlingua Creek trickles across the valley floor until merging with the Rio Grande. However, during thunderstorms, the creek's churning waters join forces with the Rio Grande to create powerful floods. The Chisos Mountains dominate the eastern horizon while tilted layers of the Aguja Formation form the small hills to the east and southeast. The Aguja layers were deformed by the Terlingua Fault, the same fault that exposed the Cretaceous **limestone** layers and enabled the ancestral Rio Grande to cut Santa Elena Canyon. The Terlinqua Fault is located in the **talus** at the base of the large cliff to your left.

1.00

1.50 **Slow down area**.
Dark-colored **igneous** rocks crop out to the north- northwest (left). These **basalts** lie on Cretaceous-age **Javelina Formation** sediments.

1.20

2.70 **Slow down area**.
The road to Terlingua Abaja goes west at this point. Stay on Maverick Road.

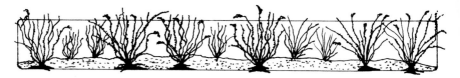

*Crossbedding,
mile 2.80.*

*White selenite crystals,
mile 2.80.*

Remnants of the Chisos Formation igneous rocks remain around the Terlingua Abaja area.

.10

2.80 **Stop 2** – Park on the right.
Here the Cretaceous-age Aguja Formation crops out as layers of **sandstones, siltstones,** and **mudstones.** Walk among the mounds adjacent to the road and observe the **crossbedding** and ripple marks in the sandstone beds. An occasional fossilized shell pokes out of the sediment, a reminder of the marine life of ancient Big Bend. Combined, · these features tell geologists that the Aguja Formation probably formed in a **"near-shore" environment,** analogous to modern day beaches and tidal flats.

Scattered about on the ground lie glimmering crystals of **gypsum.** These **secondary minerals** formed recently in response to evaporation. The gypsum occurs as large clear mineral grains, **selenite,** and a powdery surface coating that looks like snow. Secondary crystals of **calcite** also fill fractures in the sandstone. The calcite, probably deposited by hot water circulating through the sandstone, formed long after the **clastic** rocks were laid down. Where did the hot water originate? Most likely, when the earth's crust permanently stretched and thinned during normal **faulting,** groundwater began circulating deeper into the hot center portion of the earth, becoming increasingly hot and accumulating elements. Upon returning to shallow crustal levels, the water travelled along fractures, cooling and depositing calcite in its wake. Although this is the most likely scenario, another possibility exists. A mass

of **magma** may have been injected into shallow levels, heating the groundwater in the immediate region. This water then may have migrated surfaceward, depositing calcite as it cooled.

From here you can catch glimpses of many of the geologic features in the park, including Santa Elena Canyon, Mule Ears, Cerro Castellan, Goat Mountain and the Chisos Mountains.

2.30

5.10 **Slow down area.**
Usually only sand and cobbles fill Alamo Creek. However, dark rumbling clouds may indicate a flash flood that will send waters rushing down the creek bed, inundating the road.

The road parallels Peña Mountain, a composite of a **Tertiary**-age igneous **intrusion** protecting Cretaceous-age sediments.

.90

6.00 **Stop 3** – Park on the right.
Nestled at the base of Peña Mountain stands Luna's Jacal, home to an early farming family. Look for the bold **contact** between the intrusion and the sediments displayed in the face of the mountain. A "baked zone" (reddish-orange) marks the contact between the two units, formed when the hot intrusion worked its way through the sediment and literally cooked the clastic rocks in its path. If you scramble up the side of Peña Mountain you will quickly see the different textures exhibited by the intrusion, sediments and contact zone rocks and can begin to appreciate how erosion can more easily destroy one rock type than another.

Peña Mountain.

Different rock textures exhibited by the intrusion at the base of Pena Mountain, mile 6.00.

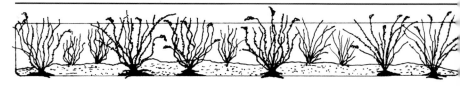

.20

6.20 **Slow down area**.
Directly ahead is Tule Mountain. The layered rocks exposed in the flanks of this mountain are **lava** and **tuffs** of the Chisos Formation.

.20

6.40 **Slow down area,** Chimneys Trailhead.
The trail can be a very pleasant 7-mile wintertime hike if transportation can be arranged on the opposite end. For more details consult the *Hiker's Guide to the Trails of Big Bend National Park* published by the Big Bend Natural History Association.

.10

6.50 Alamo Creek Crossing

.25

6.75 **Slow down area**.
Exposed on the right side of the road, about 100 yards away, is a narrow slice of the Javelina Formation sandstone.

.55

7.30 **Slow down area**.
Crossbedded sandstones of the Aguja Formation crop out on the left side of the road.

.50

7.80 **Slow down area**.
The colorful sedimentary rocks east of the

road are part of the Javelina Formation. The colors formed as **weathering** destroyed the original minerals, leaving behind red and orange iron oxides and black manganese oxide stains.

.60

8.40 **Stop 4** – Park on the right.
The road passes between outcrops of the Aguja Formation on the left side of the road and the Javelina Formation on the right. Notice how the color of the road surface changes. The yellow surface is the Aguja Formation while the grayish-purple surface is the Javelina Formation. These Cretaceous-age strata, dominantly mudstones, display examples of typical **badlands** topography. Being quite uniform in composition, the layers of mudstone erode similarly. Because of this characteristic when rain pelts the outcrops no preferential drainage pattern forms. Instead water incises numerous pathways into the rock creating small peaks and deep channels. This gives rise to the **"hummocky"** appearance displayed by these hills. Several good examples of badlands topography await you on the remainder of the trip.

.40

8.80 **Slow down area**.
The road cuts through a **pediment** carved into the Javelina Formation. Observe the contact between the Cretaceous-age rock forming the outcrop foundation and the thin sheet of alluvial cover. It is easy to confuse an **alluvial fan** and a pediment surface at first, as both are common and similar desert landforms. Remember

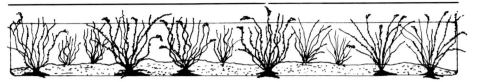

though, that alluvial fans form by deposition of material while pediments form by erosion.

1.10

9.90 **Stop 5** – Park on the right, get out of your vehicle and walk to the right.

This stop provides a vista of features both inside and outside the park. To the north stands the Tertiary-age rhyolitic intrusion of Maverick Mountain. To the northeast the Chisos Mountains are visible with Tule Mountain in the immediate foreground.

Walk up the slope to the right and enjoy the truly spectacular view. The dark Alamo Creek Basalt lies over the Cretaceous-age Javelina sediments covering the valley floor. A red-brown "baked zone" marks the contact between the two units. Volcanic material once filled the valley. Water carved through the tuffs and ash, carrying huge volumes of rock material to the Rio Grande. Now only remnants of the Chisos Formation tuffs remain, lining the valley walls.

Look at the dark rocks at your feet. These are part of the Ash Spring Basalt. Carefully examine a fragment of this basalt and note the glassy black mineral grains of **pyroxene** and the larger white to yellow crystals of **plagioclase feldspar**. These common and quite distinctive minerals frequently occur in basalts.

2.80

12.70 **Slow down area.**

You have reached the intersection of Maverick Road and the main park road. Reflect on the variety of erosional landscapes that you encountered on this journey: pediments, badlands topography, and **differential erosion**. Weathering has added color to these landforms, painting them with iron and manganese stains. Erosion slowly sculpts and shapes the ever changing face of the Big Bend country.

Panther Junction to Persimmon Gap

Persimmon Gap.

Panther Junction to Persimmon Gap

Panther Junction to Persimmon Gap
(Suggested travel time: late afternoon)
28.10 miles one way

The drive from Park Headquarters at Panther Junction to Persimmon Gap can be considered a journey back through geologic time. The mountains behind the Visitor Center are made up of **Tertiary**-age **igneous** rocks. Farther to the north, the **Cretaceous**-age **sedimentary** rocks were deposited by the streams from which dinosaurs drank. Around Persimmon Gap, the **Paleozoic**-age deep sea sediments have been deformed by the mountain building forces that marked the collision of North America and South America long ago. These rocks tell us of the dramatic geologic changes that have occurred in Big Bend during the past several hundred million years. What is now desert was once the deep sea off the edge of the continent. Later mountains dominated the area and were then eroded, leaving us no record of events for that time. Once more a shallow sea covered the area in Late Cretaceous time and gradually it withdrew, being replaced by swamps and marshlands. Again, mountains formed, and in the late stages of their development, fiery volcanoes spewed their **ash** and **lava** over the landscape. Finally the land was broken by faults and the ground shuddered as earthquakes shook the area. As quiet returned, erosion became the dominant process and the present landforms evolved.

Throughout this drive, try to envision what the area looked like millions and hundreds of millions of years ago. This will give you a deeper understanding of the story written and preserved in the rocks.

Mileage Reading
0.00 Set odometer at mile marker zero and travel north toward Persimmon Gap.

1.70

1.70 **Stop 1** — Park on shoulder.
Exposed on each side of the road is a special type of intrusive igneous rock called a **ring dike**. It probably formed when the major volcano that formed the Pine Canyon **caldera** collapsed after erupting large amounts of lava and ash.

The rocks of this ring dike reveal two minerals present as large grains: clear quartz and chalky white alkali **feldspar**. These minerals crystallized and grew in the magma when it was held beneath the Earth's surface. The holes in the rock, called **vesicles,** formed when the cooling and solidifying magma captured gas bubbles; each hole represents a pocket of trapped gas. Not everything in the rocks is original, though. Some of the vesicles contain **secondary minerals** of quartz and

Lone Mountain.

Ring dike displaying two different jointing patterns, platey and columnar, mile 1.70.

calcite formed as groundwater circulated through the solidified dike, leaching some elements from the rock and precipitating new minerals, such as calcite. Water also deposited the iron and manganese oxides as orange, brown, and black stains on the surfaces of the rocks. Some of the stains appear as concentric bands of color, termed **liesegang banding**.

On the right side of the road, the ring dike displays two different jointing patterns: **columnar** and **platey**. Columnar joints form when magma cools and shrinks rather quickly, while platey joints form when mineral crystals become aligned and more or less parallel as magma flows. By examining these joints, you not only discover the magmatic history of the ring dike, but can also determine groundwater pathways by tracing the colorful iron and manganese oxide staining.

Another ring dike, visible to the southwest, is Lone Mountain. It too has prominent columnar jointing indicating that it cooled near the surface. The talus slope of columns blanketing Lone Mountain shows the relative ease with which erosional forces have attacked and broken them apart.

1.70

3.40 **Slow down area**.
To the left are **alluvial** deposits, a continual reminder that **erosion** is the dominant geologic force in the Big Bend area today. Heavy summer thunderstorms swell streams and strip away rock fragments from the banks. Water deposits these fragments on the valley floor as alluvial material after the torrent subsides.

.60

4.00 **Stop 2** – Park on pullout. Walk the short trail to the Hannold grave site.

Across the road to the north is a good exposure of layered, or **stratified,** alluvial material. Each layer records a different episode of sediment deposition, telling us that the **alluvium** formed in many separate stages.

The trail to the grave site crosses more alluvial material. The pebbles and cobbles on the surface reflect quite a variety of rock types, clues that the streams depositing these fragments cut through different types of rocks. For example, the light-colored **carbonate** fragments probably came from the Sierra del Carmen mountains to the east while the darker pieces of igneous rock probably came from the Chisos Mountains to the south. The shapes of the fragments tell something about the history of the rocks. Angular rocks have either traveled a short distance and/or are very hard and do not readily break. Rounded rocks, on the other hand, have either been transported a great distance and/or are soft and easily shaped.

From the grave site, you can see where the stream channel has cut through older alluvial deposits. Again, the layering in the **alluvium** indicates that the rocks were deposited in several different episodes. The tall trees and shrubs near the grave site herald the presence of a desert spring. These springs are frequently associated with alluvial deposits- alluvium is **permeable** and **porous**. Consequently, rain water easily percolates through the alluvium until it encounters a barrier, for example, clay. Unable to drain further into the ground, the water is then funneled to the surface.

The abundant alluvium in these lowlands catches and stores enormous quantities of water, causing springs to flow months after the last rainfall.

Compare the two headstones at the grave site. The more recent one is cut from marble that had to be shipped from another locality. However, in the early history of the region settlers often made do with local materials. For example, the older headstone is actually hewn from rock taken from one of the ring dikes.

In the foreground to the east are the reddish brown intrusive rocks that form the McKinney Hills. Behind these are the Cretaceous-age sedimentary rocks of the Sierra del Carmen.

1.10

5.10 **Slow down area**.
The road goes downhill, cutting through a well stratified **alluvial fan**.

.20

5.30 **Slow down area**.
The sedimentary rocks on either side of the road are part of the Canoe Formation, deposited early in the Tertiary period, before the volcanoes in Big Bend became active.

.50

5.80 **Stop 3** – Park on shoulder.
The Canoe Formation consists of both **sandstones** and **siltstones**. These rock types are termed **clastic,** meaning they formed from the fragmentation of preexisting rocks. Sands are typically found in beach environments. As surf worked this

Canoe Formation,
mile 6.80.

ancient shoreline, it removed the very small particles and left behind larger sand and silt-size grains. Time and pressure transformed these particles into the sandstones and siltstones seen today. At this particular stop most of the rocks are sandstones with some parts of the outcrop thick and massive while others are quite thinbedded. At the northeast part of the roadcut look for a small exposure of siltstone; it is much finer-grained than the sandstone. The rocks deposited here reflect the vast environmental changes that have taken place in the Big Bend, ranging from the wave washed beaches of the early Tertiary to the sun parched desert of today.

1.00

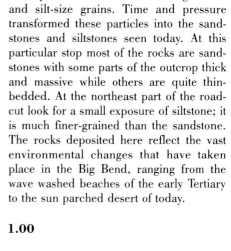

Hannold Hill Forma-
tion, mile 6.80.

6.80 **Stop 4** — Park on shoulder.
There are both Canoe and Hannold Hill Formations exposed at this stop. The dark sandstones of the Canoe Formation capping the low hills are crossbedded, probably resulting from the action of ancient water currents. Red, yellow and brown siltstones of the Hannold Hill lie beneath the sandstones. Since these two different types of sedimentary rocks lie one on top of one another, it indicates a change in the Tertiary environment. Geologists believe that the sea level was dropping during this time, a process called **regression**. As the seas retreated, the lagoon or tidal flat environment indicated by the siltstones of the Hannold Hill gave way to the beach environment suggested by the Canoe Formation.

58

Panther Junction to Persimmon Gap

.40

7.20 **Stop 5** – Park on shoulder.
The small hills to the right of the road (approximately 300 feet (100 meters away)) are being supported by a dike. The **basaltic** dike contains yellow to clear colored, striated mineral grains of **plagioclase feldspar**. The highest hill in that group, mosaic-like in appearance, exhibits a wide range of colors ranging from dark gray to yellow-brown to orange. Despite the color change, only one type of rock is present. The color variation is produced solely by the chemical breakdown of different minerals in the rock. The hill still stands because the dike has more successfully resisted erosion than the surrounding rocks. Nonetheless, **weathering** and erosion have exacted a toll on the dike. Its minerals are breaking down to form **clays** and pieces of the dike are being broken and removed. As long as the dike remains exposed to the forces of erosion, it will continue to disintegrate. Although erosion may seem destructive, it is the breakdown of rock that produces new soil, thus helping to sustain plant and animal life.

.20

7.40 **Stop 6** – Park on shoulder.
The purplish green to tan siltstones of the Hannold Hill Formation on the immediate left produce picturesque desertscapes. The colorful appearance of these rolling hills is influenced by the type and amount of minerals that are present in each layer. Iron-rich minerals weather to shades of yellow and orange and manganese-rich minerals, to purple and black.
    The eroding Hannold Hill Formation displays another geologic feature: a **dendritic** or branching drainage pattern. When a rock is fairly uniform, like this siltstone, water drainages develop in one direction as easily as another, producing the branching pattern you see here. In effect, this outcrop is an example of small-scale **badlands** topography. Look for other occurrences of the badlands topography during your travels through Big Bend.

.60

8.00 Bridge across Upper Tornillo Creek.

.25

8.25 **Stop 7** – Turn to the right at the Fossil Bone Exhibit. Note odometer reading and adjust mileage upon return to main road. Walk to exhibit.
    The Hannold Hill Formation appears again on the short walk to the fossil bone exhibit. The crossbedding in some of the outcrops suggests that a current, either of water or wind, produced this pattern. It is often difficult to ascertain whether water or wind originally deposited and shaped a sandstone unit. But a clue to the origin of this sandstone deposit can be found at the top of the overlook where a thin layer of **conglomerate** is bedded within the sandstone. The conglomerate contains rounded pebbles indicating that moving water tumbled, smoothed, and polished the stones. Although dinosaur and mammal bones have been found in the cretaceous-age Aguja and Javelina Formations, only mammal bones have been found in the Tertiary-age Hannold Hill and Black Peaks Formations.
    Why didn't the dinosaurs survive into

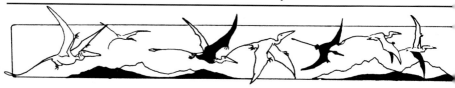

the Tertiary? Geologists propose several theories to account for the disappearance of dinosaurs at the end of the Cretaceous period. Some speculate that the increasing population of mammals both ate dinosaur eggs and competed with dinosaurs for the same food.

Recently, other scientists have begun to support the notion that a large meteorite struck the Earth, forming huge clouds of debris into the atmosphere. This debris blackened the sky, cooling the Earth enough to inhibit plant growth. The smaller mammals, needing less food than the gigantic dinosaurs, were more successful in surviving this disaster than the ill-fated dinosaurs.

How would scientists go about testing this kind of theory? The answer may lie in the presence of the element iridium in the layers of sediment at the Cretaceous-Tertiary boundary. Although iridium, one of the platinum group metals, is quite rare on Earth, it is relatively common in meteorites. If a large meteorite had impacted the Earth, the resulting debris cloud, containing iridium, would have ultimately settled through the atmosphere and been incorporated in the sediment. Geologists are now looking closely at the late-Cretaceous, early-Tertiary sedimentary layers in Big Bend, especially the Javelina and Black Peaks Formations, to determine if high concentrations of iridium are present. If abundant iridium is found world-wide at the Cretaceous-Tertiary boundary, the meteorite theory may well prove to be correct.

But the reason that dinosaurs became extinct may never be completely understood. Theories such as meteorite impact

are just that: theories. Scientists must use available facts and evidence to develop and test theories. The Big Bend region is proving to be an excellent natural laboratory for studying the enigma of dinosaur extinction.

(Note: Mileage resumes at the main road).

.15

8.40 **Stop 8** – Park on shoulder.
The hills in the foreground to the left are again composed of the Hannold Hill Formation, consisting primarily of sandstone above, and siltstone, below. See Stop 6 where the Hannold Hill Formation is first introduced. Through water and wind erosion, the softer siltstone has been cut away undermining the harder sandstone caprock. This phenomenon, an excellent example of differential erosion, will eventually lead to the collapse of the sandstone caprock. The effects of differential erosion appear time and time again in the park.

On the east side of the road is another exposure of the Hannold Hill Formation. Do you notice any crossbedding in this outcrop? Does this exposure of the Hannold Hill differ from the one at the Fossil Bone exhibit?

The hills in the left background are the Rosillos Mountains, formed from an igneous intrusion.

.75

9.15 **Slow down area.**
Watch for exposures of sandstones and siltstones of the Black Peaks Formation appearing on both sides of the road.

Panther Junction to Persimmon Gap

.90

10.05 **Slow down area**.
On the right side of the road are sandstones of the Black Peaks Formation. The dark shiny coating on the rocks is referred to as **desert varnish**. Composed of manganese and iron oxides, desert varnish forms when water evaporates from a rock's surface, leaving behind the black and brown colored oxides. Geologists have recently discovered that waste products from microorganisms living on the rocks may contribute additional manganese oxide to the desert varnish. The longer a rock is exposed, the thicker and darker the coating of varnish becomes.

Sandstones of the Black Peaks Formation, mile 10.05.

.95

11.00 **Stop 9** – Park on shoulder.
The Cretaceous-age Javelina Formation in the distance is one of the major formations that yields dinosaur bones. Exposed on both sides of the road, best seen to the right, this formation displays a variety of color patterns ranging from green to buff to purple. The same factors controlling rock color at Stop 6 influence color here, too. But these rocks tell a more dramatic geologic story than that of mere color. The rock layers are tilting or **dipping** to the southwest at about 12 degrees. Geologists know sedimentary rocks are originally deposited as horizontal layers. However these rocks have been buckled by compressive forces, creating a series of **anticlines** and **synclines**. This anticline formed during the **Laramide Orogeny**, approximately 60 million years ago.

Javelina Formation in the foreground, mile 11.00.

Panther Junction to Persimmon Gap

*Fossilized log on
Tornillo Flat.*

1.30

12.30 **Slow down area**.
The buff-colored rocks to the left, a mixture of sandstones, siltstones and mudstones, are exposures of the Cretaceous-age Aguja Formation. Paleontologists sifting through the Aguja have unearthed dinosaur bones just as they have in the Javelina Formation. The types of rocks and fossils found in the Aguja Formation and Javelina Formations are characteristic of marsh and swamplands, suggesting to geologists that the now arid Big Bend country was much wetter and cooler during the Cretaceous period.

2.00

14.30 **Slow down area**.
The panorama along this relatively straight stretch of road is evidence of the tremendous geologic diversity that exists here. The Rosillos Mountains, due west, and flat-topped Santiago Peak, slightly north of the Rosillos, are examples of Tertiary-age igneous rocks. Straight ahead is Dagger Mountain, composed of several Cretaceous-age sedimentary units, including the Santa Elena Limestone and Del Rio Clay, both laid down in shallow seas. The Dagger Mountain anticline formed when forces in the Earth lifted and bent the Cretaceous rocks during the Laramide Orogeny. The prominent notch halfway between Dagger Mountain and Santiago Peak is Persimmon Gap, through which the road passes. Exposed there are the oldest rocks in the park.

*Rosillos Mountains,
mile 14.30.*

Panther Junction to Persimmon Gap

1.30

15.60 **Slow down area**.
In the arroyo on the left side of the road the layered Boquillas Formation dips to the west. The beds are oriented this way because they lie on the western flank of the Sierra Del Carmen Anticline. (Note: This outcrop is not easily seen if you are heading south towards Park Headquarters).

1.40

17.00 **Slow down area**.
The layers of rock visible to the right on Dagger Mountain appear to dip to the north but the beds on the back side dip toward the south. Folding of the rock produced these different orientations. In effect, you are seeing both sides of the anticline at once. It took millions of years for the compressive forces associated with the Laramide Orogeny to fold these sedimentary rocks into the Dagger Mountain anticline.

4.50

21.50 **Stop 10** – Park on pullout.
At this stop, there is direct evidence that water is a major process affecting landscape evolution today. Flood waters rushing down arroyos and drainages have cut rectangular-shaped stream channels and box canyons before seeping into the desert floor. The large rocks left standing in the stream bed and exposed in the channel walls show the power of water on the rampage.

From this stop, the Rosillos Mountains are in full view. The igneous rocks of the Rosillos lie on top of, and parallel to the sedimentary rocks of the Pen Formation.

Boquillas Formation,
mile 15.60.

Rosillos Mountains,
mile 21.50.

Flash flood,
mile 21.50.

When contacts between an intrusive rock and the original (country) rock are parallel, geologists say that the contact is **concordant**. The presence of the concordant contact here argues for the Rosillos intrusion being either a **laccolith** or a large **sill**. Dikes, such as the ring dikes you saw earlier, cut through country rock and are said to have a **discordant** contact.

.60

22.10 **Slow down area**.
In the foreground to the right of the road, limestones of the Boquillas Formation are exposed. The characteristically thin-bedded Boquillas limestone, sometimes called a **flagstone,** is influencing the distribution of plants here. Look at the small hills of flagstone and note how the vegetation grows parallel to the beds of limestone rather than in·a random pattern across the entire outcrop.

1.00

Dog Canyon,
mile 23.10.

23.10 **Stop 11** — Park on pullout.
In addition to telling about the U.S. Army's use of camels in the desert, this stop affords the opportunity to observe evidence of very old and very recent geologic processes. Dog Canyon, located to the east and consisting of intensely folded rocks, records the influence of the Laramide Orogeny. Erosive forces have cut through the rock forming Dog Canyon, providing us with an excellent view of the twisted rocks.

On the slopes of the Santiago Mountains, to the right, a much more recent geologic event is recorded. The massive limestones of the Santa Elena Formation make up the cliff face of the mountains.

The other Cretaceous-age units beneath the Santa Elena Formation form slopes, indicating that they are more easily eroded than the cliff-forming limestones.

The large scar on the cliff face resulted from a landslide that occurred in the spring of 1987. The softer slope-forming rocks were removed by erosion, thus undercutting the Santa Elena limestone to a point that the unsupported cliff collapsed, sending boulders of limestone crashing down the slope. This type of erosion, termed **mass wasting**, has occurred in the Santiago Mountains before. To the right of the recent slide are scars left by earlier landslide events. This landslide scar will be visible well into the next century.

1987 landslide, mile 23.10.

The small hill on the left side of the road is composed primarily of the Cretaceous-age Aguja Formation and is capped by an intrusive igneous rock. Like the Rosillos Mountains, this intrusion displays a concordant contact, so it should correctly be termed a sill.

1.90

25.00 **Slow down area**.
To the left of the road lies a classic concordant contact of columnar jointing between the Aguja and the intrusion of the previous stop.

.80

25.80 **Slow down area**.
On the right side of the road are outcrops of the Cretaceous-age Aguja, Pen and Del Rio Clay Formations. These units appear so similar at first glance that even a geologist may be confused by the various formations.

Outcrops of various clay formations, mile 26.00.

Tesnus Formation,
mile 26.70.

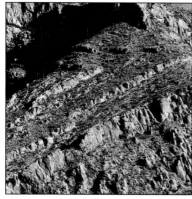

Folded rocks of the
Caballos Formation,
mile 26.70.

.90

26.70 **Stop 12** — Visitor Center at Persimmon Gap.

A short walk up the stream bed on the right side of the road affords a close look at the oldest rocks in the park. As in any desert hike, be sure to carry water. The trek passes the highly bent and contorted beds of the Paleozoic- age Tesnus, Maravillas and Caballos Formations. These formations are difficult to distinguish. In general, however, the Tesnus consists of sandstones and green cherts; the Maravillas Formation has gray to black limestones and black chert; and the Caballos Formation is dominantly a white chert.

A dramatic and ancient geologic story is revealed in these rocks. The Tesnus, Maravillas and Caballos Formations, originally deposited as horizontal layers of sediment in the ocean, were buried and sustained enormous amounts of pressure, In time, it transformed them into sedimentary rocks. During the Ouachita Orogeny (more than 250 million year ago) internal forces folded and lifted these rocks high above the ocean basin. Imagine picking up a piece of chert and trying to bend it into a different form, obviously an impossible task. However, the orogenic forces that continued for millions of years were successful in reshaping these Paleozoic rocks. Once these forces began to wane, erosion attacked the newly formed mountains. During the Cretaceous, seas once again engulfed this region and new layers of sediment covered the folded Paleozoic strata. The geologic story repeated itself because

the new sediments were also transformed into sedimentary rocks: the Pen, Aguja, Del Rio Clay, Glen Rose and Santa Elena Formations. As in the Paleozoic, a period of intense uplift and folding, the Laramide Orogeny, created mountains from rocks once held in the sea floor.

The light-colored cliffs here are part of the Glen Rose Formation. The Laramide Orogeny caused these limestones to be folded and thrust on top of the older Paleozoic rocks. One such fold is well preserved and exposed in the southern cliff face.

.60

27.30 **Slow down area.**
Outcrops of the Tesnus Formation can be seen to the rear right.

.80

28.10 **Stop 13** — Park on pullout on the left, the boundary of Big Bend National Park.
Stop and recall the wide variety of geology and geologic processes encountered today. They range from recent alluvial fans and landslides — products of modern erosional processes — to rocks more than 400 million years old. You walked on sedimentary rocks that hold remains of dinosaurs that once reigned supreme during the Cretaceous period. The dikes, sills, and laccoliths you saw are tangible reminders of past igneous activity. Clearly, no one geologic process has dominated in what is now Big Bend National Park. The glimpses of Big Bend's geologic past are only a sampling of the possible geologic future. With time, the high mountains we now see will be leveled and even deeper canyons will be cut. Perhaps in the distant geologic future seas will once again cover this region, hiding for a moment this land's geologic treasures. One thing is certain: more change is inevitable. It can only enhance the already intriguing geologic history of Big Bend National Park.

Glossary of Geologic Terms

Air fall tuffs	Compacted pyroclastic material erupted into the atmosphere and settling to the surface in more or less parallel layers.
Aguja Formation	A Cretaceous-age sedimentary unit that consists of sandstones, silts and clays. Dinosaur bones and fossilized wood are found in this formation.
Alluvial	Composed of alluvium.
Alluvial fan	A fan-shaped erosional deposit of sand and gravel found at the base of steep slopes.
Alluvium	Stream carved deposits of sediments such as flood- plains or alluvial fans.
Anticline	A fold in which the oldest rocks are found in the center; normally this is a convex structure.
Ash	Uncemented, fine-grained pyroclastic material extruded from volcanoes and calderas.
Badlands	Rugged and highly eroded topography, nearly devoid of vegetation, produced in relatively unconsolidated material by stream erosion so that a maze of sharp ravines and crests is formed.
Bajada	The feature produced when two or more alluvial fans merge.
Basalt	A common extrusive igneous rock that is usually dark gray to black in color. It frequently contains plagioclase feldspar and/or pyroxene phenocrysts.
Basanite	A mafic rock that contains less silica than a basalt.
Basin and Range Faulting	Normal faults that break an area into a series of tilted fault blocks. The downdropped edge of the blocks are the basins and the upturned edges are the ranges.
Breccia	Fragmental rocks whose components are angular in contrast to conglomerates which are waterworn.
Burrows	A cylindrical tube made by a mud-eating worm or mollusk.
Caballos Formation	A Paleozoic formation composed of sedimentary rocks. Frequently this formation is recognized by its thick, white chert beds.
Calcite	The most common calcium carbonate mineral. Often forms beautiful crystals in the park.
Caldera	A large, roughly circular depression formed when enormous volumes of magma are removed from the magma chamber of a volcano which collapses.
Caliche	A secondary deposit of calcium carbonate that is usually seen as a white surface coating in arid regions.

Caprock	A resistant rock layer that covers or caps a softer rock layer thus protecting the softer unit from erosion.
Carbonate	A chemical sedimentary rock that is composed primarily of minerals such as calcite, limestone and dolomite.
Chert	A chemical sedimentary rock consisting mainly of silica, similar to flint.
Cenozoic	The most recent era of geologic time (see *Introduction*, p. 9).
Clastic	Rock or sediment that is composed of fragments derived from preexisting rock.
Clay	A group of finely crystalline, hydrous-silicate minerals that are layered. Clays frequently form from the breakdown of other minerals.
Columnar	Parallel polygonal columns that form in some joints of intrusive and extrusive rocks as they cool.
Concordant	Describes the parallel (non-crosscutting) contact between an intrusive rock and the rock it intrudes.
Conglomerate	A clastic sedimentary rock composed of cemented rounded particles, generally larger than 2 mm, often with a fine-grained matrix.
Contact	The interface between two rock units.
Cretaceous	The last period of geologic time that occurred during the Mesozoic era. This period of time was the last one in which dinosaurs were present (see *Introduction*, p. 9).
Crossbedding	Layers of sedimentary units are laid down at angles to each other rather than horizontally.
Deep marine	Deeper parts of the ocean, including ocean basins; these areas are generally not affected by normal tide or wave action.
Delta	The nearly flat, fan-shaped, alluvial deposit that is commonly found at the mouths of rivers.
Dendritic	A random branching pattern resembling a tree that can be produced by surface drainage in a rock that erodes uniformly.
Desert varnish	A thin, dark surface coating composed primarily of iron and manganese oxides found on rocks in arid regions.
Differential erosion	Breakdown of rock that occurs at different rates due to the variable resistance of different rock types.
Dike	A tabular intrusive rock which cuts across pre- existing layers of rock.
Dip	The angle that a rock layer makes with a horizontal plane.

Dipping	A rock layer which has been tilted from the horizontal position.
Discordant	Used to describe the cross-cutting (non-parallel) contact an intrusive rock makes with the pre-existing rocks.
Dolomite	A calcium and magnesium carbonate mineral.
Eon	An indefinitely long period of time. Generally speaking, this can represent more than one era of geologic time.
Exfoliation	A weathering process where thin, concentric slabs of rocks are removed from an outcrop. It may also be caused by release of confining pressure. Responsible for rounded shape of granite boulders.
Erosion	The wearing down and removal of rock material and soil by a number of processes including wind, running water, weathering, and mass wasting.
Extrusive	A volcanic rock that is erupted onto the earth's surface, such as lava flows, ash flows and tuffs.
Faulting	The movement which produces relative displacement of adjacent rock units along a fracture.
Feldspar	A group of aluminum silicate minerals, usually containing sodium, potassium or calcium; commonly found in igneous rocks. Feldspars weather into clays.
Flagstone	A rock that splits readily into slabs.
Float	A piece of rock found lying on the surface of the earth. Generally, the rock unit from which it came is not evident.
Fluvial	Pertaining to the processes and products produced by stream and river action.
Folding	The bending of a rock or layers of rock due to external pressures.
Graben	A down-dropped block of crustal material that is bounded by faults.
Graptolites	Extinct Paleozoic marine tube-shaped organisms that built small colonies of chitinous material. Their fossils look like pencil marks, hence the name.
Gypsum	A calcium sulfate mineral. Forms clear, translucent or sometimes transparent crystals that can easily be identified because they can be scratched with a fingernail.
Hornfels	A fine-grained unfoliated rock formed by contact metamorphism.
Horst	An uplifted block of crustal material that is bounded by faults.
Hummocky	Referring to a series of low, rounded hills.

Hydrothermal	Pertaining to the effects of hot water and the products, such as mineralization, which accompany its circulation.
Igneous	Pertaining to rocks, either intrusive or extrusive, that were produced by melting of material beneath the surface.
Intrusion	A rock mass formed when molten rock cools and solidifies beneath the surface, often after infiltrating an area of existing rock.
Iridium	Element number 77 in the periodic chart, considered to be one of the platinum group of metals, believed to be associated with meteorite impact.
Jacal	A Spanish word for a small hut or hovel constructed mainly of rocks and adobe.
Javelina Formation	A Cretaceous-age sedimentary unit that is younger than the Aguja Formation. The Javelina Formation has colorful beds of mudstones and siltstones interbedded with sandstone layers.
Joint	A fracture in a rock that does not have any movement (displacement) along it.
Jurassic	A period of geologic time that occurred in the Mesozoic era (see *Introduction*, p. 9).
Laccolith	A mushroom-shaped, concordant intrusive rock that has pushed the overlying rocks which it has intruded, into a dome, and which has a floor.
Laramide	An intense period of mountain building (the Laramide Orogeny) that occurred at the close of the Cretaceous period.
Lava	Molten rock that is extruded onto the earth's surface.
Lava flow	An outpouring of molten rock on top of the ground.
Liesegang banding	Concentric rings or bands of color produced in a rock by weathering.
Limestone	A chemical sedimentary rock that consists primarily of calcium carbonate minerals.
Lithified	Refers to a process that converts unconsolidated sediments, by heat and/or pressure, into rock.
Mafic	A dark colored rock, such as basalt, that is rich in iron and magnesium minerals.
Magma	Molten rock found originating beneath the surface of the earth.
Maravillas	A Paleozoic rock formation composed of sedimentary rock units, as in the Maravillas Formation.
Mass-wasting	The movement of rock material downslope in response to gravity.

71

Member	A distinct subgroup of rock types that occur together as part of a rock formation.
Meteorite	A solid rock-like object that falls from space and lands on the earth.
Mesozoic	The era of geologic time preceding the latest era (see *Introduction*, p. 9).
Monolithic	A rock mass composed of one kind of rock, especially when it is shaped like a pillar or is found in a cliff.
Mudflow	A general term used for the transport of material by a fine-grained, water-rich sediment.
Mudstone	A clastic sedimentary rock that is composed of particles that are less than 1/256th of a mm in size.
Near shore environment	Area of the ocean that is found near the environment shoreline.
Orogeny	The processes involved in the formation of mountains; mountain building by folding and faulting.
Ouachita	A time of mountain building that occurred near the close of the Paleozoic, as in the Ouachita Orogeny.
Paleoclimate	Climate that was present in the geologic past.
Paleozoic	The oldest era of geologic time containing common fossils (see *Introduction*, p. 8).
Pediment	A gently sloping erosional surface cut into solid rock layers that is usually covered with a thin layer of alluvial gravel.
Permeable	The quality that allows fluids or gasses to move through sediment or rock.
Phenocryst	A large mineral grain or crystal that is easily visible with the naked eye in a porphyritic igneous rock.
Plagioclase feldspar	An aluminum silicate mineral frequently found in igneous rocks that contains potassium, sodium, and/or calcium.
Plate	A rigid segment of the Earth which includes the crust and uppermost mantle.
Platey	The appearance of a rock when it readily breaks into thin, tabular pieces.
Plug	Relatively small intrusive body of igneous rock which can represent a filled volcanic conduit.
Porous	Containing holes or pores.
Porphyritic	A texture used to describe an igneous rock that has larger phenocrysts housed in a fine-grained groundmass.
Precambrian	The whole of geologic time from the very beginning of earth history until the earliest fossiliferous Cambrian beds.

Pyroclastic	Used to describe clastic rock material that is exploded into the air by a volcano.
Pyroxene	An iron-magnesium bearing silicate mineral that is frequently found in igneous rocks.
Radiometric	The age of a rock that is determined by the age radioactive decay of a parent isotope to its daughter isotope; e.g. potassium 40 (parent) decaying to argon 40 (daughter).
Regression	The retreat of an ocean from the land masses.
Rhyolite	A fine-grained igneous rock that is rich in silica frequently has minerals of both quartz and alkali feldspar present.
Ring dike	A dike that is more or less circular; these sometimes form in response to caldera collapse.
Rubbly	The appearance of an outcrop when rock fragments are dislodged and scattered on the surface.
Sandstone	A clastic sedimentary rock consisting of particles that are dominantly 1/16 to 2 mm in size (sand size).
Sheet flow	A type of flow in which the stream surfaces remain distinct from one another over their entire length.
Secondary minerals	Minerals that form at a later date than the rock minerals they are found in.
Sediment	An accumulation of solid material made up of particles that settle from a liquid.
Sedimentary	Rock containing sediment formed from the breakdown of preexisting rock material, referred to as clastic or by chemical precipitation from solution, referred to as chemical. Includes sandstones, limestone and chert.
Shale	A laminated, fine-grained clastic sedimentary rock whose particles are less than 1/256th of a mm in size.
Silica	A product of chert and quartz, the most common chemical component on earth.
Silica-rich	Used to describe an igneous rock that is rich in silicon dioxide (Si 02) such as rhyolite.
Sill	A tabular intrusive rock that is intruded parallel to pre-existing rock layers.
Siltstone	A clastic sedimentary rock that consists primarily of particles 1/256 to 1/16 mm in size (silt size).
Spheroidal weathering	In highly fractured and jointed rocks, weathering attacks the outer edges and works towards the center. This rounds the rock edges and the rock blocks appear to weather in a rounded (spheroidal) manner.
Syenite	A coarse-textured igneous rock, rich in alkalic feldspars, common in intrusions in Big Bend National Park.

Syncline	A fold in which the youngest beds dip inward from both sides toward the axis. Ant: anticline.
Talus deposit	Rock fragments found at the base of a steep slope or cliff.
Tectonic	Pertaining to the forces within the earth that result in movement, uplift, or deformation.
Tectonic event	Any event resulting from internal earth forces that cause movement, uplift, or mountain building.
Terrigenous	Material derived from the land.
Terrestrial	Referring to the earth's land surface.
Tertiary	The earliest period of the Cenozoic era. This was a time of intense volcanism in Big Bend National Park (see *Introduction*, p. 10).
Tesnus	A Paleozoic formation composed predominately of siltstones and sandstones with some carbonate layers.
Trachyandesite	A type of igneous rock that is intermediate in composition between trachyte and andesite. In Big Bend, the Tule Mountain Trachyandesite is an example.
Triassic	A period of geologic time that occurred in the Mesozoic era (see *Introduction*, p. 9).
Tuffs	Compacted pyroclastic material, usually ash deposits.
Unconformity	A time gap in the rock record, caused by erosion or nondeposition, evident when one rock unit is overlaid by another rock unit that is considerably younger.
Unlithified	Loose sediments that have not been transformed into solid rock.
Uplift	The raising of a crustal block by tectonic forces.
Vesicle	A small, circular cavity in igneous rock formed by the expansion of a bubble of gas or steam during the solidification of rock.
Volcaniclastic	A rock unit that consists of volcanic fragments; generally, these fragments have been reworked by water since their original deposition.
Volcanism	Any of the processes by which magma makes it way to the surface and is either erupted as lava or into the atmosphere as ash. Volcanism is derived from Vulcan, the mythological Roman god of fire and craftsmanship.
Weathering	The physical and chemical breakdown of rocks to sediments, through processes such as rainfall, freezing and thawing, wind, plant action, etc.
Welded	The consolidation of fine-grained pyroclastic material through heat and pressure.

REFERENCES CITED
AND SUGGESTED READING

Barker, D.S., Henry, C.D. and McDowell, F.W., 1986, Pine Canyon Caldera, Big Bend National Park: a mildly peralkaline magmatic system: In: J.G. Price, C. D. Henry, D.F. Parker and D.S. Barker (eds): Igneous Geology of Trans-Pecos Texas, Field Trip Guide and Research Articles: The University of Texas at Austin, Bureau of Economic Geology Guidebook 23, pp.

Cameron, M., Cameron, K.L. and Carman, M.F., 1986, Alkaline Rocks in the Terlingua-Big Bend Area of Trans-Pecos, Texas: In: J.G. Price, C.D. Henry, D.F. Parker and D.S. Barker (eds): Igneous Geology of Trans-Pecos Texas, Field Trip Guide and Research Articles; The University of Texas at Austin, Bureau of Economic Geology Guidebook 23, pp. 123-142.

Chesser, K. and Estepp, J.D., 1986, Hot Springs of Big Bend National Park and Trans-Pecos Texas: In: P.H. Pause and R.G. Spears, (eds.), Geology of the Big Bend Area and Solitario Dome, Texas: West Texas Geological Society, Pub. 86-82, pp. 97-104.

Dasch, E.J., Armstrong, R.L. and Clabaugh, S.E., 1969, Age of Rim Rock dike swarm, Trans-Pecos Texas: Geological Society of America Bulletin, v. 80, p. 1819-1824.

Deal, D., 1979, Evolution of the Rio Conchos-Rio Grande Drainage System: In: A.W. Walton, and C.D. Henry, (eds.), Cenozoic Geology of the Trans-Pecos Volcanic Field of Texas. University of Texas Bureau of Economic Geology Guidebook 19, pp. 67-71.

Dictionary of Geologic Terms, 1984, Bates, R.L. and J.A. Jackson (eds.), Prepared under the direction of The American Geological Institute: Anchor Press/Doubleday, New York, 571 p.

Ehlers, E.G. and Blatt, H., 1982, Petrology: Igneous, Metamorphic and Sedimentary. W.H. Freeman and Company, San Francisco, 732 p.

Henry, C.D. 1979, Crustal Structure Deduced from Geothermal Studies, Trans-Pecos Texas: In: A.W. Walton, and C.D. Henry, (eds.), Cenozoic Geology of the Trans-Pecos Volcanic Field of Texas. University of Texas Bureau of Economic Geology Guidebook 19, pp. 67-71.

Henry, C.D. and McDowell, F.W., 1986, Geochronology of magmatism in the Tertiary Volcanic Field, Trans-Pecos, Texas: In: J.G. Price, C.D. Henry, D.F. Parker and D.S. Baker (eds): Igneous Geology of Trans-Pecos Texas, Field Trip Guide and Research Articles: The University of Texas at Austin, Bureau of Economic Geology Guidebook 23, pp. 99- 122.

Henry, C.D. and Price, J.G., 1984, Variations in Caldera Development in the Tertiary Volcanic Field of Trans-Pecos Texas: In: Calderas and Associate Igneous Rocks, Journal of Geophysical Research, v. 89, no. B10, p. 8765-8786.

Hyndman, D.W., 1985, Petrology of Igneous and Metamorphic Rocks: McGraw-Hill, New York, 786 p.

King, P.B., 1935, Outline of Structural Development of Trans- Pecos Texas, American Association of Petroleum Geologists, Bull. Vol. 19, pp. 256-261.

Langston, W., Jr, 1986, Rebuilding the World's Biggest Flying Creature: the second coming of Quetzalcoatlus northropi: In: P.H. Pause and R.G. Spears, (eds,), Geology of the Big Bend Area and Solitario Dome, Texas: West Texas Geological Society, Pub. 86-82, pp. 125-128.

Maxwell, R.A., 1968, The Big Bend of the Rio Grande: A guide to the Rocks, Landscape, Geologic History and Settlers of the Area of Big Bend National Park. University of Texas Bureau of Economic Geology Guidebook 7, 138 p.

Maxwell R.A., Lonsdale, J.T., Hazzard, R.T. and Wilson, J.A., 1967, Geology of Big Bend National Park, Texas: University of Texas Bureau of Economic Geology Publication 6711, 320 p.

Nelson, D.O., Nelson, K.L., Reeves, K.D. and Mattison, G.D. 1987, Geochemistry of Tertiary Alkaline Rocks of the Eastern Trans-Pecos Magmatic Province, Texas. Contributions to Mineralogy and Petrology, v. 97, pp. 72-92.

Nelson, D.O. and Nelson, K.L., 1986, Evolution of Igneous Rocks in the Trans-Pecos Magmatic Province: In: P.H. Pause and R.G. Spears, (eds.), Geology of the Big Bend Area and Solitario Dome, Texas: West Texas Geological Society, Pub. 86-82,pp. 143-149.

Ogley, D.S. 1979, Eruptive History of the Pine Canyon Caldera, Big Bend Park: In: A.W. Walton, and C.D. Henry, (eds.), Cenozoic Geology of the Trans-Pecos Volcanic Field of Texas. University of Texas Bureau of Economic Geology Guidebook 19, pp. 67-71.

Pettijohn, F.J., 1975, Sedimentary Rocks, Harper and Row, New York, 628 p.

Plummer, C.C. and McGeary, D., 1988, Physical Geology. Wm. C. Brown, Iowa, 535 p.

Price, J.G. and Henry, C.D., 1984, Stress Orientations during Oligocene Volcanism in Trans-Pecos, Texas: timing and transition from Laramide compression to Basin and Range extension, Geology, v. 12, p. 238-241.

Tauvers, P.R. and Muehlberger, W.R., Persimmon Gap In Big Bend National Park, Texas: Ouachita facies and Cretaceous cover in a Laramide overthrust. GSA Centennial Field Guide South-Central Section, in press.